T0257354

C# 12 Pocket Reference
Instant Help for C# 12
Programmers

Joseph Albahari and Ben Albahari

Beijing · Boston · Farnham · Sebastopol · Tokyo

C# 12 Pocket Reference

by Joseph Albahari and Ben Albahari

Published by O'Reilly Media, Inc., 1005 Gravenstein Highway North, Sebastopol, CA 95472.

O'Reilly books may be purchased for educational, business, or sales promotional use. Online editions are also available for most titles (*https://oreilly.com*). For more information, contact our corporate/institutional sales department: 800-998-9938 or *corporate@oreilly.com*.

Acquisitions Editor: Brian Guerin
Development Editor: Sarah Grey
Production Editor: Kristen Brown
Copyeditor: Charles Roumeliotis
Proofreader: Piper Editorial Consulting, LLC
Indexer: WordCo Indexing Services, Inc.
Interior Designer: David Futato
Cover Designer: Karen Montgomery
Illustrator: Kate Dullea

November 2023:   First Edition

Revision History for the First Edition
          2023-10-27:   First Release

See *https://oreil.ly/c12prERR* for release details.

978-1-098-14754-9

[LSI]

Table of Contents

Table of Contents

C# 12 Pocket Reference

C# is a general-purpose, type-safe, primarily object-oriented programming language, the goal of which is programmer productivity. To this end, the language balances simplicity, expressiveness, and performance. C# 12 is designed to work with the Microsoft *.NET 8* runtime (whereas C# 11 targets .NET 7, C# 10 targets .NET 6, and C# 7 targets Microsoft *.NET Framework* 4.6/4.7/4.8).

NOTE

The programs and code snippets in this book mirror those in Chapters 2 through 4 of *C# 12 in a Nutshell* and are all available as interactive samples in *LINQPad* (*http://www.linqpad.net*). Working through these samples in conjunction with the book accelerates learning in that you can edit the samples and instantly see the results without needing to set up projects and solutions in Visual Studio.

To download the samples, click the Samples tab in LINQPad and then click "Download more samples." LINQPad is free—go to *www.linqpad.net*.

A First C# Program

Following is a program that multiplies 12 by 30 and prints the result, 360, to the screen. The double forward slash indicates that the remainder of a line is a *comment*:

```
int x = 12 * 30;                    // Statement 1
System.Console.WriteLine (x);       // Statement 2
```

Our program consists of two *statements*. Statements in C# execute sequentially and are terminated by a semicolon. The first statement computes the *expression* 12 * 30 and stores the result in a *variable*, named x, whose type is a 32-bit integer (int). The second statement calls the WriteLine *method* on a *class* called Console, which is defined in a *namespace* called System. This prints the variable x to a text window on the screen.

A method performs a function; a class groups function members and data members to form an object-oriented building block. The Console class groups members that handle command-line input/output (I/O) functionality, such as the WriteLine method. A class is a kind of *type*, which we examine in "Type Basics" on page 8.

At the outermost level, types are organized into *namespaces*. Many commonly used types—including the Console class—reside in the System namespace. The .NET libraries are organized into nested namespaces. For example, the System.Text namespace contains types for handling text, and System.IO contains types for input/output.

Qualifying the Console class with the System namespace on every use adds clutter. The using directive lets you avoid this clutter by *importing* a namespace:

```
using System;                  // Import the System namespace

int x = 12 * 30;
Console.WriteLine (x);    // No need to specify System
```

A basic form of code reuse is to write higher-level functions that call lower-level functions. We can *refactor* our program with a reusable *method* called FeetToInches that multiplies an integer by 12, as follows:

```
using System;

Console.WriteLine (FeetToInches (30));     // 360
Console.WriteLine (FeetToInches (100));    // 1200

int FeetToInches (int feet)
{
  int inches = feet * 12;
  return inches;
}
```

Our method contains a series of statements surrounded by a pair of braces. This is called a *statement block*.

A method can receive *input* data from the caller by specifying *parameters* and *output* data back to the caller by specifying a *return type*. Our FeetToInches method has a parameter for inputting feet, and a return type for outputting inches:

```
int FeetToInches (int feet)
...
```

The *literals* 30 and 100 are the *arguments* passed to the Feet ToInches method.

If a method doesn't receive input, use empty parentheses. If it doesn't return anything, use the void keyword:

```
using System;
SayHello();

void SayHello()
{
  Console.WriteLine ("Hello, world");
}
```

Methods are one of several kinds of functions in C#. Another kind of function we used in our example program was the * *operator*, which performs multiplication. There are also *constructors*, *properties*, *events*, *indexers*, and *finalizers*.

Compilation

The C# compiler compiles source code (a set of files with the *.cs* extension) into an *assembly*. An assembly is the unit of packaging and deployment in .NET. An assembly can be either an *application* or a *library*. A normal console or Windows application has an *entry point*, whereas a library does not. The purpose of a library is to be called upon (*referenced*) by an application or by other libraries. .NET itself is a set of libraries (as well as a runtime environment).

Each of the programs in the preceding section began directly with a series of statements (called *top-level statements*). The presence of top-level statements implicitly creates an entry point for a console or Windows application. (Without top-level statements, a *Main method* denotes an application's entry point—see "Symmetry of predefined types and custom types" on page 10.)

To invoke the compiler, you can either use an integrated development environment (IDE) such as Visual Studio or Visual Studio Code, or call it manually from the command line. To manually compile a console application with .NET, first download the .NET 8 SDK, and then create a new project, as follows:

```
dotnet new console -o MyFirstProgram
cd MyFirstProgram
```

This creates a folder called *MyFirstProgram*, which contains a C# file called *Program.cs*, which you can then edit. To invoke the compiler, call `dotnet build` (or `dotnet run`, which will compile and then run the program). The output will be written to a subdirectory under *bin\debug*, which will include *MyFirstProgram.dll* (the output assembly) as well as *MyFirstProgram.exe* (which runs the compiled program directly).

Syntax

C# syntax is inspired by C and C++ syntax. In this section, we describe C#'s elements of syntax, using the following program:

```
using System;

int x = 12 * 30;
Console.WriteLine (x);
```

Identifiers and Keywords

Identifiers are names that programmers choose for their classes, methods, variables, and so on. Here are the identifiers in our example program, in the order in which they appear:

```
System   x   Console   WriteLine
```

An identifier must be a whole word, essentially made up of Unicode characters starting with a letter or underscore. C# identifiers are case sensitive. By convention, parameters, local variables, and private fields should be in *camel case* (e.g., myVariable), and all other identifiers should be in *Pascal case* (e.g., MyMethod).

Keywords are names that mean something special to the compiler. There are two keywords in our example program, using and int.

Most keywords are *reserved*, which means that you can't use them as identifiers. Here is the full list of C# reserved keywords:

abstract	event	new	string
as	explicit	null	struct
base	extern	object	switch
bool	false	operator	this
break	finally	out	throw
byte	fixed	override	true
case	float	params	try
catch	for	private	typeof
char	foreach	protected	uint
checked	goto	public	ulong
class	if	readonly	unchecked
const	implicit	record	unsafe
continue	in	ref	ushort
decimal	int	return	using
default	interface	sbyte	virtual
delegate	internal	sealed	void
do	is	short	volatile
double	lock	sizeof	while
else	long	stackalloc	
enum	namespace	static	

Avoiding conflicts

If you really want to use an identifier that clashes with a reserved keyword, you can do so by qualifying it with the @ prefix. For instance:

```
class class  {...}      // Illegal
class @class {...}      // Legal
```

The @ symbol doesn't form part of the identifier itself. So @myVariable is the same as myVariable.

Contextual keywords

Some keywords are *contextual*, meaning they can also be used as identifiers—without an @ symbol. The contextual keywords are as follows:

add	file	nameof	required
alias	from	nint	select
and	get	not	set
ascending	global	notnull	unmanaged
async	group	nuint	value
await	init	on	var
by	into	or	with
descending	join	orderby	when
dynamic	let	partial	where
equals	managed	remove	yield

With contextual keywords, ambiguity cannot arise within the context in which they are used.

Literals, Punctuators, and Operators

Literals are primitive pieces of data lexically embedded into the program. The literals we used in our example program are 12 and 30. *Punctuators* help demarcate the structure of the program. An example is the semicolon, which terminates a statement. Statements can wrap multiple lines:

```
Console.WriteLine
    (1 + 2 + 3 + 4 + 5 + 6 + 7 + 8 + 9 + 10);
```

An *operator* transforms and combines expressions. Most operators in C# are denoted with a symbol, such as the multiplication operator, *. Here are the operators in our program:

```
= * . ()
```

A period denotes a member of something (or a decimal point with numeric literals). Parentheses are used when declaring or calling a method; empty parentheses are used when the method accepts no arguments. The equals sign performs *assignment* (the double equals sign, ==, performs equality comparison).

Comments

C# offers two different styles of source code documentation: *single-line comments* and *multiline comments*. A single-line comment begins with a double forward slash and continues until the end of the line. For example:

```
int x = 3;    // Comment about assigning 3 to x
```

A multiline comment begins with /* and ends with */. For example:

```
int x = 3;    /* This is a comment that
                 spans two lines */
```

Comments can embed XML documentation tags (see "XML Documentation" on page 258).

Type Basics

A *type* defines the blueprint for a value. In our example, we used two literals of type int with values 12 and 30. We also declared a *variable* of type int whose name was x.

A *variable* denotes a storage location that can contain different values over time. In contrast, a *constant* always represents the same value (more on this later).

All values in C# are an *instance* of a specific type. The meaning of a value, and the set of possible values a variable can have, is determined by its type.

Predefined Type Examples

Predefined types (also called *built-in* types) are types that are specially supported by the compiler. The int type is a predefined type for representing the set of integers that fit into 32 bits of memory, from -2^{31} to $2^{31}-1$. We can perform functions such as arithmetic with instances of the int type as follows:

```
int x = 12 * 30;
```

Another predefined C# type is string. The string type represents a sequence of characters, such as ".NET" or "*http://oreilly.com*". We can work with strings by calling functions on them, as follows:

```
string message = "Hello world";
string upperMessage = message.ToUpper();
Console.WriteLine (upperMessage);        // HELLO WORLD

int x = 2022;
message = message + x.ToString();
Console.WriteLine (message);             // Hello world2022
```

The predefined bool type has exactly two possible values: true
and false. The bool type is commonly used to conditionally
branch execution flow with an if statement. For example:

```
bool simpleVar = false;
if (simpleVar)
  Console.WriteLine ("This will not print");

int x = 5000;
bool lessThanAMile = x < 5280;
if (lessThanAMile)
  Console.WriteLine ("This will print");
```

The System namespace in .NET contains many important types
that are not predefined by C# (e.g., DateTime).

Custom Type Examples

Just as you can build complex functions from simple functions,
you can build complex types from primitive types. In this
example, we will define a custom type named UnitConverter—
a class that serves as a blueprint for unit conversions:

```
UnitConverter feetToInches = new UnitConverter (12);
UnitConverter milesToFeet = new UnitConverter (5280);

Console.WriteLine (feetToInches.Convert(30));    // 360
Console.WriteLine (feetToInches.Convert(100));   // 1200
Console.WriteLine (feetToInches.Convert
                     (milesToFeet.Convert(1)));  // 63360


public class UnitConverter
{
  int ratio;                          // Field

  public UnitConverter (int unitRatio)  // Constructor
```

```
    {
      ratio = unitRatio;
    }

    public int Convert (int unit)          // Method
    {
      return unit * ratio;
    }
  }
```

Members of a type

A type contains *data members* and *function members*. The data member of UnitConverter is the *field* called ratio. The function members of UnitConverter are the Convert method and the UnitConverter's *constructor*.

Symmetry of predefined types and custom types

A beautiful aspect of C# is that predefined types and custom types have few differences. The predefined int type serves as a blueprint for integers. It holds data—32 bits—and provides function members that use that data, such as ToString. Similarly, our custom UnitConverter type acts as a blueprint for unit conversions. It holds data—the ratio—and provides function members to use that data.

Constructors and instantiation

Data is created by *instantiating* a type. You can instantiate predefined types simply by using a literal such as 12 or "Hello world".

The new operator creates instances of a custom type. We started our program by creating two instances of the UnitConverter type. Immediately after the new operator instantiates an object, the object's *constructor* is called to perform initialization. A constructor is defined like a method, except that the method name and return type are reduced to the name of the enclosing type:

```
public UnitConverter (int unitRatio)   // Constructor
{
  ratio = unitRatio;
}
```

Instance versus static members

The data members and function members that operate on the *instance* of the type are called *instance members*. UnitConverter's Convert method and int's ToString method are examples of instance members. By default, members are instance members.

Data members and function members that don't operate on the instance of the type can be marked as static. To refer to a static member from outside its type, you specify its *type* name rather than an *instance*. An example is the WriteLine method of the Console class. Because this is static, we call Console.Write Line() and not new Console().WriteLine().

In the following code, the instance field Name pertains to an instance of a particular Panda, whereas Population pertains to the set of all Panda instances. We create two instances of the Panda, print their names, and then print the total population:

```
Panda p1 = new Panda ("Pan Dee");
Panda p2 = new Panda ("Pan Dah");

Console.WriteLine (p1.Name);       // Pan Dee
Console.WriteLine (p2.Name);       // Pan Dah

Console.WriteLine (Panda.Population);    // 2

public class Panda
{
  public string Name;               // Instance field
  public static int Population;      // Static field

  public Panda (string n)           // Constructor
  {
    Name = n;                       // Instance field
    Population = Population + 1;     // Static field
  }
}
```

Attempting to evaluate `p1.Population` or `Panda.Name` will generate a compile-time error.

The public keyword

The `public` keyword exposes members to other classes. In this example, if the `Name` field in `Panda` was not marked as public, it would be private and could not be accessed from outside the class. Marking a member public is how a type communicates: "Here is what I want other types to see—everything else is my own private implementation details." In object-oriented terms, we say that the public members *encapsulate* the private members of the class.

Creating a namespace

Particularly with larger programs, it makes sense to organize types into namespaces. Here's how to define the `Panda` class inside a namespace called `Animals`:

```
namespace Animals
{
  public class Panda
  {
    ...
  }
}
```

We cover namespaces in detail in "Namespaces" on page 68.

Defining a Main method

All of our examples so far have used top-level statements, a feature that was introduced in C# 9. Without top-level statements, a simple console or Windows application looks like this:

```
using System;

class Program
{
  static void Main()   // Program entry point
  {
    int x = 12 * 30;
    Console.WriteLine (x);
```

```
        }
    }
```

In the absence of top-level statements, C# looks for a static method called Main, which becomes the entry point. The Main method can be defined inside any class (and only one Main method can exist).

The Main method can optionally return an integer (rather than void) in order to return a value to the execution environment (where a nonzero value typically indicates an error). The Main method can also optionally accept an array of strings as a parameter (that will be populated with any arguments passed to the executable); for example:

```
static int Main (string[] args) {...}
```

NOTE

An array (such as string[]) represents a fixed number of elements of a particular type. Arrays are specified by placing square brackets after the element type. We describe them in "Arrays" on page 34.

(The Main method can also be declared async and return a Task or Task<int> in support of asynchronous programming—see "Asynchronous Functions" on page 235.)

Top-level statements

Top-level statements let you avoid the baggage of a static Main method and a containing class. A file with top-level statements comprises three parts, in this order:

1. (Optionally) using directives

2. A series of statements, optionally mixed with method declarations

3. (Optionally) Type and namespace declarations

Everything in Part 2 ends up inside a compiler-generated "main" method, inside a compiler-generated class. This means that the methods in your top-level statements become *local methods* (we describe the subtleties in "Local methods" on page 75). Top-level statements can optionally return an integer value to the caller, and access a "magic" variable of type string[] called args, corresponding to command-line arguments passed by the caller.

As a program can have only one entry point, there can be at most one file with top-level statements in a C# project.

Types and Conversions

C# can convert between instances of compatible types. A conversion always creates a new value from an existing one. Conversions can be either *implicit* or *explicit*: implicit conversions happen automatically, whereas explicit conversions require a *cast*. In the following example, we *implicitly* convert an int to a long type (which has twice the bit capacity of an int) and *explicitly* cast an int to a short type (which has half the bit capacity of an int):

```
int x = 12345;      // int is a 32-bit integer
long y = x;         // Implicit conversion to 64-bit int
short z = (short)x; // Explicit conversion to 16-bit int
```

In general, implicit conversions are allowed when the compiler can guarantee that they will always succeed without loss of information. Otherwise, you must perform an explicit cast to convert between compatible types.

Value Types Versus Reference Types

C# types can be divided into *value types* and *reference types*.

Value types comprise most built-in types (specifically, all numeric types, the `char` type, and the `bool` type) as well as custom `struct` and `enum` types. *Reference types* comprise all class, array, delegate, and interface types.

The fundamental difference between value types and reference types is how they are handled in memory.

Value types

The content of a *value type* variable or constant is simply a value. For example, the content of the built-in value type `int` is 32 bits of data.

You can define a custom value type with the `struct` keyword (see Figure 1):

```
public struct Point { public int X, Y; }
```

Figure 1. A value type instance in memory

The assignment of a value type instance always *copies* the instance. For example:

```
Point p1 = new Point();
p1.X = 7;

Point p2 = p1;              // Assignment causes copy

Console.WriteLine (p1.X);   // 7
Console.WriteLine (p2.X);   // 7

p1.X = 9;                   // Change p1.X
Console.WriteLine (p1.X);   // 9
Console.WriteLine (p2.X);   // 7
```

Figure 2 shows that p1 and p2 have independent storage.

Figure 2. Assignment copies a value type instance

Reference types

A reference type is more complex than a value type, having two parts: an *object* and the *reference* to that object. The content of a reference type variable or constant is a reference to an object that contains the value. Here is the Point type from our previous example rewritten as a class (see Figure 3):

```
public class Point { public int X, Y; }
```

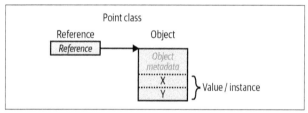

Figure 3. A reference type instance in memory

Assigning a reference type variable copies the reference, not the object instance. This allows multiple variables to refer to the same object—something that's not ordinarily possible with value types. If we repeat the previous example, but with Point now a class, an operation via p1 affects p2:

```
Point p1 = new Point();
p1.X = 7;

Point p2 = p1;              // Copies p1 reference

Console.WriteLine (p1.X);   // 7
Console.WriteLine (p2.X);   // 7
```

```
p1.X = 9;                    // Change p1.X
Console.WriteLine (p1.X);    // 9
Console.WriteLine (p2.X);    // 9
```

Figure 4 shows that p1 and p2 are two references that point to the same object.

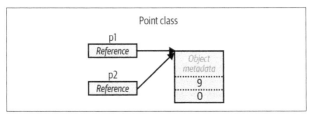

Figure 4. Assignment copies a reference

Null

A reference can be assigned the literal null, indicating that the reference points to no object. Assuming Point is a class:

```
Point p = null;
Console.WriteLine (p == null);   // True
```

Accessing a member of a null reference generates a runtime error:

```
Console.WriteLine (p.X);   // NullReferenceException
```

NOTE

In "Nullable Reference Types" on page 172, we describe a feature of C# that reduces accidental NullReference Exception errors.

In contrast, a value type cannot ordinarily have a null value:

```
struct Point {...}
...
Point p = null; // Compile-time error
int x = null;   // Compile-time error
```

To work around this, C# has a special construct for representing value-type nulls—see "Nullable Value Types" on page 167.

Predefined Type Taxonomy

The predefined types in C# are as follows:

Value types
- Numeric:
  - — Signed integer (sbyte, short, int, long)
  - — Unsigned integer (byte, ushort, uint, ulong)
  - — Real number (float, double, decimal)
- Logical (bool)
- Character (char)

Reference types
- String (string)
- Object (object)

Predefined types in C# alias .NET types in the System namespace. There is only a syntactic difference between these two statements:

```
int i = 5;
System.Int32 i = 5;
```

The set of predefined *value* types excluding decimal are known as *primitive types* in the Common Language Runtime (CLR). Primitive types are so called because they are supported directly via instructions in compiled code, which usually translates to direct support on the underlying processor.

Numeric Types

C# has the following predefined numeric types:

C# type	System type	Suffix	Size	Range
Integral—signed				
sbyte	SByte		8 bits	-2^7 to 2^7-1
short	Int16		16 bits	-2^{15} to $2^{15}-1$
int	Int32		32 bits	-2^{31} to $2^{31}-1$
long	Int64	L	64 bits	-2^{63} to $2^{63}-1$
nint	IntPtr		32/64 bits	
Integral—unsigned				
byte	Byte		8 bits	0 to 2^8-1
ushort	UInt16		16 bits	0 to $2^{16}-1$
uint	UInt32	U	32 bits	0 to $2^{32}-1$
ulong	UInt64	UL	64 bits	0 to $2^{64}-1$
nuint	UIntPtr		32/64 bits	
Real				
float	Single	F	32 bits	$\pm(\sim 10^{-45}$ to $10^{38})$
double	Double	D	64 bits	$\pm(\sim 10^{-324}$ to $10^{308})$
decimal	Decimal	M	128 bits	$\pm(\sim 10^{-28}$ to $10^{28})$

Of the *integral* types, int and long are first-class citizens and are favored by both C# and the runtime. The other integral types are typically used for interoperability or when space efficiency is paramount. The nint and nuint native-sized integer types are sized to match the address space of the process at runtime (32 or 64 bits). These types can be useful when working with pointers—we describe their nuances in Chapter 4 of *C# 12 in a Nutshell* (O'Reilly).

Of the *real* number types, float and double are called *floating-point types* and are typically used for scientific and graphical calculations. The decimal type is typically used for financial calculations where base-10-accurate arithmetic and high precision are required. (Technically, decimal is a floating-point type, too, although it's not generally referred to as such.)

Numeric Literals

Integral-typed literals can use decimal, hexadecimal, or binary notation; hexadecimal is denoted with the 0x prefix (e.g., 0x7f is equivalent to 127), and binary is denoted with the 0b prefix. *Real literals* can use decimal or exponential notation such as 1E06. Underscores may be inserted within (or before) a numeric literal to improve readability (e.g., 1_000_000).

Numeric literal type inference

By default, the compiler *infers* a numeric literal to be either double or an integral type:

- If the literal contains a decimal point or the exponential symbol (E), it is a double.

- Otherwise, the literal's type is the first type in this list that can fit the literal's value: int, uint, long, and ulong.

For example:

```
Console.Write (        1.0.GetType()); // Double (double)
Console.Write (      1E06.GetType()); // Double (double)
Console.Write (         1.GetType()); // Int32  (int)
Console.Write (0xF0000000.GetType()); // UInt32 (uint)
Console.Write (0x100000000.GetType()); // Int64  (long)
```

Numeric suffixes

The *numeric suffixes* listed in the preceding table explicitly define the type of a literal:

```
decimal d = 3.5M;   // M = decimal (case-insensitive)
```

The suffixes U and L are rarely necessary because the uint, long, and ulong types can nearly always be either *inferred* or *implicitly converted* from int:

```
long i = 5;      // Implicit conversion from int to long
```

The D suffix is technically redundant in that all literals with a decimal point are inferred to be double (and you can always add a decimal point to a numeric literal). The F and M suffixes are the most useful and are mandatory when you're specifying fractional float or decimal literals. Without suffixes, the following would not compile because 4.5 would be inferred to be of type double, which has no implicit conversion to float or decimal:

```
float f = 4.5F;       // Won't compile without suffix
decimal d = -1.23M;   // Won't compile without suffix
```

Numeric Conversions

Integral-to-integral conversions

Integral conversions are *implicit* when the destination type can represent every possible value of the source type. Otherwise, an *explicit* conversion is required. For example:

```
int x = 12345;         // int is a 32-bit integral type
long y = x;            // Implicit conversion to 64-bit int
short z = (short)x;    // Explicit conversion to 16-bit int
```

Real-to-real conversions

A float can be implicitly converted to a double because a double can represent every possible float value. The reverse conversion must be explicit.

Conversions between decimal and other real types must be explicit.

Real-to-integral conversions

Conversions from integral types to real types are implicit, whereas the reverse must be explicit. Converting from a floating-point to an integral type truncates any fractional portion; to perform rounding conversions, use the static System.Convert class.

A caveat is that implicitly converting a large integral type to a floating-point type preserves *magnitude* but might occasionally lose *precision*:

```
int i1 = 100000001;
float f = i1;      // Magnitude preserved, precision lost
int i2 = (int)f;   // 100000000
```

Arithmetic Operators

The arithmetic operators (+, -, *, /, %) are defined for all numeric types except the 8- and 16-bit integral types. The % operator evaluates the remainder after division.

Increment and Decrement Operators

The increment and decrement operators (++, --, respectively) increment and decrement numeric types by 1. The operator can either precede or follow the variable, depending on whether you want the variable to be updated *before* or *after* the expression is evaluated. For example:

```
int x = 0;
Console.WriteLine (x++);   // Outputs 0; x is now 1
Console.WriteLine (++x);   // Outputs 2; x is now 2
Console.WriteLine (--x);   // Outputs 1; x is now 1
```

Specialized Integral Operations

Division

Division operations on integral types always eliminate the remainder (round toward zero). Dividing by a variable whose value is zero generates a runtime error (a DivideByZeroException). Dividing by the *literal* or *constant* 0 generates a compile-time error.

Overflow

At runtime, arithmetic operations on integral types can overflow. By default, this happens silently—no exception is thrown, and the result exhibits wraparound behavior, as though the computation were done on a larger integer type and the extra significant bits discarded. For example, decrementing the minimum possible int value results in the maximum possible int value:

```
int a = int.MinValue; a--;
Console.WriteLine (a == int.MaxValue); // True
```

The checked and unchecked operators

The checked operator instructs the runtime to generate an OverflowException rather than overflowing silently when an integral-typed expression or statement exceeds the arithmetic limits of that type. The checked operator affects expressions with the ++, --, (unary) -, +, -, *, /, and explicit conversion operators between integral types. Overflow checking incurs a small performance cost.

You can use checked around either an expression or a statement block. For example:

```
int a = 1000000, b = 1000000;

int c = checked (a * b);   // Checks just the expression

checked                    // Checks all expressions
{                          // in statement block
   c = a * b;
   ...
}
```

You can make arithmetic overflow checking the default for all expressions in a program by compiling with the /checked+ command-line switch (in Visual Studio, go to Advanced Build Settings). If you then need to disable overflow checking just for specific expressions or statements, you can do so with the unchecked operator.

Bitwise operators

C# supports the following bitwise operators:

Operator	Meaning	Sample expression	Result
~	Complement	~0xfU	0xfffffff0U
&	And	0xf0 & 0x33	0x30
|	Or	0xf0 | 0x33	0xf3
^	Exclusive Or	0xff00 ^ 0x0ff0	0xf0f0
<<	Shift left	0x20 << 2	0x80
>>	Shift right	0x20 >> 1	0x10

From C# 11, there is also an unsigned shift-right operator (>>>). Whereas the shift-right operator (>>) replicates the high-order bit when operating on signed integers, the unsigned shift-right operator (>>>) does not.

8- and 16-Bit Integral Types

The 8- and 16-bit integral types are byte, sbyte, short, and ushort. These types lack their own arithmetic operators, so C# implicitly converts them to larger types as required. This can cause a compilation error when trying to assign the result back to a small integral type:

```
short x = 1, y = 1;
short z = x + y;          // Compile-time error
```

In this case, x and y are implicitly converted to int so that the addition can be performed. This means that the result is also an int, which cannot be implicitly cast back to a short (because it could cause loss of data). To make this compile, you must add an explicit cast:

```
short z = (short) (x + y);   // OK
```

Special Float and Double Values

Unlike integral types, floating-point types have values that certain operations treat specially. These special values are NaN (Not a Number), +∞, −∞, and −0. The `float` and `double` classes have constants for NaN, +∞, and −∞ (as well as other values including `MaxValue`, `MinValue`, and `Epsilon`). For example:

```
Console.Write (double.NegativeInfinity);   // -Infinity
```

Dividing a nonzero number by zero results in an infinite value:

```
Console.WriteLine ( 1.0 /  0.0);   //  Infinity
Console.WriteLine (-1.0 /  0.0);   // -Infinity
Console.WriteLine ( 1.0 / -0.0);   // -Infinity
Console.WriteLine (-1.0 / -0.0);   //  Infinity
```

Dividing zero by zero, or subtracting infinity from infinity, results in a NaN:

```
Console.Write ( 0.0 / 0.0);                 //  NaN
Console.Write ((1.0 / 0.0) - (1.0 / 0.0));  //  NaN
```

When you use ==, a NaN value is never equal to another value, even another NaN value. To test whether a value is NaN, you must use the `float.IsNaN` or `double.IsNaN` method:

```
Console.WriteLine (0.0 / 0.0 == double.NaN);   // False
Console.WriteLine (double.IsNaN (0.0 / 0.0));  // True
```

When you use `object.Equals`, however, two NaN values are equal:

```
bool isTrue = object.Equals (0.0/0.0, double.NaN);
```

double Versus decimal

`double` is useful for scientific computations (such as computing spatial coordinates). `decimal` is useful for financial computations and values that are manufactured rather than the result of real-world measurements. Here's a summary of the differences:

Feature	double	decimal
Internal representation	Base 2	Base 10
Precision	15–16 significant figures	28–29 significant figures
Range	$\pm(\sim10^{-324}$ to $\sim10^{308})$	$\pm(\sim10^{-28}$ to $\sim10^{28})$
Special values	$+0$, -0, $+\infty$, $-\infty$, and NaN	None
Speed	Native to processor	Non-native to processor (about 10 times slower than double)

Real Number Rounding Errors

float and double internally represent numbers in base 2. For this reason, most literals with a fractional component (which are in base 10) will not be represented precisely, making them bad for financial calculations. In contrast, decimal works in base 10 and so can precisely represent fractional numbers such as 0.1 (whose base-10 representation is nonrecurring).

Boolean Type and Operators

C#'s bool type (aliasing the System.Boolean type) is a logical value that can be assigned the literal true or false.

Although a Boolean value requires only one bit of storage, the runtime will use one byte of memory because this is the minimum chunk that the runtime and processor can efficiently work with. To avoid space inefficiency in the case of arrays, .NET provides a BitArray class in the System.Collec tions namespace that is designed to use just one bit per Boolean value.

Equality and Comparison Operators

`==` and `!=` test for equality and inequality, respectively, of any type and always return a `bool` value. Value types typically have a very simple notion of equality:

```
int x = 1, y = 2, z = 1;
Console.WriteLine (x == y);      // False
Console.WriteLine (x == z);      // True
```

For reference types, equality, by default, is based on *reference*, as opposed to the actual *value* of the underlying object. Therefore, two instances of an object with identical data are not considered equal unless the `==` operator for that type is specially overloaded to that effect (see "The object Type" on page 106 and "Operator Overloading" on page 226).

The equality and comparison operators, `==`, `!=`, `<`, `>`, `>=`, and `<=`, work for all numeric types but should be used with caution with real numbers (see "Real Number Rounding Errors" on page 26 in the previous section). The comparison operators also work on `enum` type members by comparing their underlying integral values.

Conditional Operators

The `&&` and `||` operators test for *and* and *or* conditions, respectively. They are frequently used in conjunction with the `!` operator, which expresses *not*. In the following example, the `UseUmbrella` method returns `true` if it's rainy or sunny (to protect us from the rain or the sun), as long as it's not also windy (because umbrellas are useless in the wind):

```
static bool UseUmbrella (bool rainy, bool sunny,
                         bool windy)
{
  return !windy && (rainy || sunny);
}
```

The `&&` and `||` operators *short-circuit* evaluation when possible. In the preceding example, if it is windy, the expression `(rainy || sunny)` is not even evaluated. Short-circuiting is essential in allowing expressions such as the following to run without throwing a `NullReferenceException`:

```
if (sb != null && sb.Length > 0) ...
```

The & and | operators also test for *and* and *or* conditions:

```
return !windy & (rainy | sunny);
```

The difference is that they *do not short-circuit*. For this reason, they are rarely used in place of conditional operators.

The ternary conditional operator (simply called the *conditional operator*) has the form q ? a : b, where if condition q is true, a is evaluated, otherwise b is evaluated. For example:

```
static int Max (int a, int b)
{
  return (a > b) ? a : b;
}
```

The conditional operator is particularly useful in LINQ queries.

Strings and Characters

C#'s char type (aliasing the System.Char type) represents a Unicode character and occupies two bytes (UTF-16). A char literal is specified inside single quotes:

```
char c = 'A';        // Simple character
```

Escape sequences express characters that cannot be expressed or interpreted literally. An escape sequence is a backslash followed by a character with a special meaning. For example:

```
char newLine = '\n';
char backSlash = '\\';
```

The escape sequence characters are as follows:

Char	Meaning	Value
\'	Single quote	0x0027
\"	Double quote	0x0022

Char	Meaning	Value
\\	Backslash	0x005C
\0	Null	0x0000
\a	Alert	0x0007
\b	Backspace	0x0008
\f	Form feed	0x000C
\n	New line	0x000A
\r	Carriage return	0x000D
\t	Horizontal tab	0x0009
\v	Vertical tab	0x000B

The \u (or \x) escape sequence lets you specify any Unicode character via its four-digit hexadecimal code:

```
char copyrightSymbol = '\u00A9';
char omegaSymbol     = '\u03A9';
char newLine         = '\u000A';
```

An implicit conversion from a char to a numeric type works for the numeric types that can accommodate an unsigned short. For other numeric types, an explicit conversion is required.

String Type

C#'s string type (aliasing the System.String type) represents an immutable (unmodifiable) sequence of Unicode characters. A string literal is specified within double quotes:

```
string a = "Heat";
```

NOTE

string is a reference type rather than a value type. Its equality operators, however, follow value type semantics:

```
string a = "test", b = "test";
Console.Write (a == b);  // True
```

The escape sequences that are valid for char literals also work within strings:

```
string a = "Here's a tab:\t";
```

The cost of this is that whenever you need a literal backslash, you must write it twice:

```
string a1 = "\\\\server\\fileshare\\helloworld.cs";
```

To avoid this problem, C# allows *verbatim* string literals. A verbatim string literal is prefixed with @ and does not support escape sequences. The following verbatim string is identical to the preceding one:

```
string a2 = @"\\server\fileshare\helloworld.cs";
```

A verbatim string literal can also span multiple lines. You can include the double-quote character in a verbatim literal by writing it twice.

Raw string literals (C# 11)

Wrapping a string in three or more quote characters (""") creates a *raw string literal*. Raw string literals can contain almost any character sequence, without escaping or doubling up:

```
string raw = """<file path="c:\temp\test.txt"></file>""";
```

Raw string literals make it easy to represent JSON, XML, and HTML literals, as well as regular expressions and source code. Should you need to include three (or more) quote characters in the string itself, you can do so by wrapping the string in four (or more) quote characters:

```
string raw = """"We can include """ in this string."""";
```

Multiline raw string literals are subject to special rules. We can represent the string "Line 1\r\nLine 2" as follows:

```
string multiLineRaw = """
  Line 1
  Line 2
  """;
```

Notice that the opening and closing quotes must be on separate lines to the string content. Additionally:

- Whitespace following the *opening* """ (on the same line) is ignored.

- Whitespace preceding the *closing* """ (on the same line) is treated as *common indentation* and is removed from every line in the string. This lets you include indentation for source-code readability (as we did in our example) without that indentation becoming part of the string.

Raw string literals can be interpolated, subject to special rules described in "String interpolation" on page 31.

String concatenation

The + operator concatenates two strings:

```
string s = "a" + "b";
```

One of the operands can be a nonstring value, in which case ToString is called on that value. For example:

```
string s = "a" + 5;   // a5
```

Using the + operator repeatedly to build up a string can be inefficient; a better solution is to use the System.Text.String Builder type—this represents a mutable (editable) string and has methods to efficiently Append, Insert, Remove, and Replace substrings.

String interpolation

A string preceded with the $ character is called an *interpolated string*. Interpolated strings can include expressions within braces:

```
int x = 4;
Console.Write ($"A square has {x} sides");
// Prints: A square has 4 sides
```

Any valid C# expression of any type can appear within the braces, and C# will convert the expression to a string by calling its ToString method or equivalent. You can change the formatting by appending the expression with a colon and a *format string* (we describe format strings in Chapter 6 of *C# 12 in a Nutshell*):

```
string s = $"15 in hex is {15:X2}";
// Evaluates to "15 in hex is 0F"
```

From C# 10, interpolated strings can be constants, as long as the interpolated values are constants:

```
const string greeting = "Hello";
const string message = $"{greeting}, world";
```

From C# 11, interpolated strings are permitted to span multiple lines (whether standard or verbatim):

```
string s = $"this interpolation spans {1 +
1} lines";
```

Raw string literals (from C# 11) can also be interpolated:

```
string s = $"""The date and time is {DateTime.Now}""";
```

To include a brace literal in an interpolated string:

- With standard and verbatim string literals, repeat the desired brace character.

- With raw string literals, change the interpolation sequence by repeating the $ prefix.

Using two (or more) $ characters in a raw string literal prefix changes the interpolation sequence from one brace to two (or more) braces. Consider the following string:

```
$$"""{ "TimeStamp": "{{DateTime.Now}}" }"""
```

This evaluates to:

```
{ "TimeStamp": "01/01/2024 12:13:25 PM" }
```

String comparisons

string does not support < and > operators for comparisons. You must instead use string's CompareTo method, which returns a positive number, a negative number, or zero, depending on whether the first value comes after, before, or alongside the second value:

```
Console.Write ("Boston".CompareTo ("Austin"));   // 1
Console.Write ("Boston".CompareTo ("Boston"));   // 0
Console.Write ("Boston".CompareTo ("Chicago"));  // -1
```

Searching within strings

string's indexer returns a character at a specified position:

```
Console.Write ("word"[2]);   // r
```

The IndexOf and LastIndexOf methods search for a character within the string. The Contains, StartsWith, and EndsWith methods search for a substring within the string.

Manipulating strings

Because string is immutable, all the methods that "manipulate" a string return a new one, leaving the original untouched:

- Substring extracts a portion of a string.
- Insert and Remove insert and remove characters at a specified position.
- PadLeft and PadRight add whitespace.
- TrimStart, TrimEnd, and Trim remove whitespace.

The string class also defines ToUpper and ToLower methods for changing case, a Split method to split a string into substrings (based on supplied delimiters), and a static Join method to join substrings back into a string.

UTF-8 Strings

From C# 11, you can use the u8 suffix to create string literals encoded in UTF-8 rather than UTF-16. This feature is intended for advanced scenarios such as the low-level handling of JSON text in performance hotspots:

```
ReadOnlySpan<byte> utf8 = "ab→cd"u8;
Console.WriteLine (utf8.Length);      // 7
```

The underlying type is ReadOnlySpan<byte>, which we cover in Chapter 23 of *C# 12 in a Nutshell*. You can convert this to an array by calling the ToArray() method.

Arrays

An *array* represents a fixed number of elements of a particular type. The elements in an array are always stored in a contiguous block of memory, providing highly efficient access.

An array is denoted with square brackets after the element type. The following declares an array of five characters:

```
char[] vowels = new char[5];
```

Square brackets also *index* the array, accessing a particular element by position:

```
vowels[0] = 'a'; vowels[1] = 'e'; vowels[2] = 'i';
vowels[3] = 'o'; vowels[4] = 'u';

Console.WriteLine (vowels [1]);      // e
```

This prints "e" because array indexes start at 0. You can use a for loop statement to iterate through each element in the array. The for loop in this example cycles the integer i from 0 to 4:

```
for (int i = 0; i < vowels.Length; i++)
  Console.Write (vowels [i]);            // aeiou
```

Arrays also implement IEnumerable<T> (see "Enumeration and Iterators" on page 161), so you can also enumerate members with the foreach statement:

```
foreach (char c in vowels) Console.Write (c);  // aeiou
```

All array indexing is bounds-checked by the runtime. An `Index OutOfRangeException` is thrown if you use an invalid index:

```
vowels[5] = 'y';    // Runtime error
```

The `Length` property of an array returns the number of elements in the array. After an array has been created, its length cannot be changed. The `System.Collection` namespace and subnamespaces provide higher-level data structures, such as dynamically sized arrays and dictionaries.

An *array initialization expression* lets you declare and populate an array in a single step:

```
char[] vowels = new char[] {'a','e','i','o','u'};
```

Or simply:

```
char[] vowels = {'a','e','i','o','u'};
```

NOTE

From C# 12, you can use square brackets instead of curly braces:

```
char[] vowels = ['a','e','i','o','u'];
```

This is called a *collection expression* and has the advantage of also working when calling methods:

```
Foo (['a','e','i','o','u']);
void Foo (char[] letters) { ... }
```

Collection expressions also work with other collection types such as lists and sets—see "Collection Initializers and Collection Expressions" on page 163.

All arrays inherit from the `System.Array` class, which defines common methods and properties for all arrays. This includes instance properties such as `Length` and `Rank`, and static methods to do the following:

- Dynamically create an array (`CreateInstance`)
- Get and set elements regardless of the array type (`GetValue`/`SetValue`)
- Search a sorted array (`BinarySearch`) or an unsorted array (`IndexOf`, `LastIndexOf`, `Find`, `FindIndex`, `FindLastIndex`)
- Sort an array (`Sort`)
- Copy an array (`Copy`)

Default Element Initialization

Creating an array always preinitializes the elements with default values. The default value for a type is the result of a bitwise zeroing of memory. For example, consider creating an array of integers. Because `int` is a value type, this allocates 1,000 integers in one contiguous block of memory. The default value for each element will be 0:

```
int[] a = new int[1000];
Console.Write (a[123]);          // 0
```

With reference type elements, the default value is `null`.

An array *itself* is always a reference type object, regardless of element type. For instance, the following is legal:

```
int[] a = null;
```

Indices and Ranges

Indices and ranges (from C# 8) simplify working with elements or portions of an array.

NOTE

Indices and ranges also work with the CLR types Span<T> and ReadOnlySpan<T>, which provide efficient low-level access to managed or unmanaged memory.

You can also make your own types work with indices and ranges by defining an indexer of type Index or Range (see "Indexers" on page 85).

Indices

Indices let you refer to elements relative to the *end* of an array, with the ^ operator. ^1 refers to the last element, ^2 refers to the second-to-last element, and so on:

```
char[] vowels = new char[] {'a','e','i','o','u'};
char lastElement  = vowels[^1];   // 'u'
char secondToLast = vowels[^2];   // 'o'
```

(^0 equals the length of the array, so vowels[^0] generates an error.)

C# implements indices with the help of the Index type, so you can also do the following:

```
Index first = 0;
Index last = ^1;
char firstElement = vowels [first];   // 'a'
char lastElement = vowels [last];     // 'u'
```

Ranges

Ranges let you "slice" an array with the .. operator:

```
char[] firstTwo =  vowels [..2];   // 'a', 'e'
char[] lastThree = vowels [2..];   // 'i', 'o', 'u'
char[] middleOne = vowels [2..3];  // 'i'
```

The second number in the range is *exclusive*, so ..2 returns the elements *before* vowels[2].

You can also use the ^ symbol in ranges. The following returns the last two characters:

```
char[] lastTwo = vowels [^2..^0];    // 'o', 'u'
```

(^0 is valid here because the second number in the range is *exclusive*.)

C# implements ranges with the help of the Range type, so you can also do the following:

```
Range firstTwoRange = 0..2;
char[] firstTwo = vowels [firstTwoRange];   // 'a', 'e'
```

Multidimensional Arrays

Multidimensional arrays come in two varieties: *rectangular* and *jagged*. Rectangular arrays represent an *n*-dimensional block of memory, and jagged arrays are arrays of arrays.

Rectangular arrays

To declare rectangular arrays, use commas to separate each dimension. The following declares a rectangular two-dimensional array, where the dimensions are 3×3:

```
int[,] matrix = new int [3, 3];
```

The GetLength method of an array returns the length for a given dimension (starting at 0):

```
for (int i = 0; i < matrix.GetLength(0); i++)
  for (int j = 0; j < matrix.GetLength(1); j++)
    matrix [i, j] = i * 3 + j;
```

A rectangular array can be initialized as follows (to create an array identical to the previous example):

```
int[,] matrix = new int[,]
{
  {0,1,2},
  {3,4,5},
  {6,7,8}
};
```

(The code shown in boldface can be omitted in declaration statements such as this.)

Jagged arrays

To declare jagged arrays, use successive square-bracket pairs for each dimension. Here is an example of declaring a jagged two-dimensional array, for which the outermost dimension is 3:

```
int[][] matrix = new int[3][];
```

The inner dimensions aren't specified in the declaration because, unlike a rectangular array, each inner array can be an arbitrary length. Each inner array is implicitly initialized to null rather than an empty array. Each inner array must be created manually:

```
for (int i = 0; i < matrix.Length; i++)
{
  matrix[i] = new int [3];        // Create inner array
  for (int j = 0; j < matrix[i].Length; j++)
    matrix[i][j] = i * 3 + j;
}
```

A jagged array can be initialized as follows (to create an array identical to the previous example, but with an additional element at the end):

```
int[][] matrix = new int[][]
{
  new int[] {0,1,2},
  new int[] {3,4,5},
  new int[] {6,7,8,9}
};
```

(The code shown in boldface can be omitted in declaration statements such as this.)

Simplified Array Initialization Expressions

We've already seen how to simplify array initialization expressions by omitting the new keyword and type declaration:

```
char[] vowels = new char[] {'a','e','i','o','u'};
char[] vowels =            {'a','e','i','o','u'};
char[] vowels =            ['a','e','i','o','u'];
```

Another approach is to use the var keyword, which instructs the compiler to implicitly type a local variable. Here are some simple examples:

```
var i = 3;            // i is implicitly of type int
var s = "sausage";    // s is implicitly of type string
```

The same principle can be applied to arrays, except that it can be taken one stage further. By omitting the type qualifier after the new keyword, the compiler infers the array type:

```
// Compiler infers char[]
var vowels = new[] {'a','e','i','o','u'};
```

Here's how we can apply this to multidimensional arrays:

```
var rectMatrix = new[,]
{
  {0,1,2},
  {3,4,5},
  {6,7,8}
};
var jaggedMat = new int[][]
{
  new[] {0,1,2},
  new[] {3,4,5},
  new[] {6,7,8,9}
};
```

Variables and Parameters

A *variable* represents a storage location that has a modifiable value. A variable can be a *local variable*, *parameter* (*value*, *ref*, *out*, or *in*), *field* (*instance* or *static*), or *array element*.

The Stack and the Heap

The *stack* and the *heap* are the places where variables reside. Each has very different lifetime semantics.

Stack

The *stack* is a block of memory for storing local variables and parameters. The stack logically grows and shrinks as a method or function is entered and exited. Consider the following method (to avoid distraction, input argument checking is ignored):

```
static int Factorial (int x)
{
  if (x == 0) return 1;
  return x * Factorial (x-1);
}
```

This method is *recursive*, meaning that it calls itself. Each time the method is entered, a new int is allocated on the stack, and each time the method exits, the int is deallocated.

Heap

The *heap* is the memory in which *objects* (i.e., reference type instances) reside. Whenever a new object is created, it is allocated on the heap, and a reference to that object is returned. During a program's execution, the heap starts filling up as new objects are created. The runtime has a garbage collector that periodically deallocates objects from the heap so your program does not run out of memory. An object is eligible for deallocation as soon as it's not referenced by anything that is itself alive.

Value type instances (and object references) live wherever the variable was declared. If the instance was declared as a field within a class type, or as an array element, that instance lives on the heap.

NOTE

You can't explicitly delete objects in C# as you can in C++. An unreferenced object is eventually collected by the garbage collector.

The heap also stores static fields and constants. Unlike objects allocated on the heap (which can be garbage-collected), these live until the application domain is torn down.

Definite Assignment

C# enforces a definite assignment policy. In practice, this means that outside of an `unsafe` context, it's impossible to access uninitialized memory. Definite assignment has three implications:

- Local variables must be assigned a value before they can be read.

- Function arguments must be supplied when a method is called (unless marked optional—see "Optional parameters" on page 46).

- All other variables (such as fields and array elements) are automatically initialized by the runtime.

For example, the following code results in a compile-time error:

```
int x;                   // x is a local variable
Console.WriteLine (x);   // Compile-time error
```

The following, however, outputs 0, because fields are implicitly assigned a default value (whether instance or static):

```
Console.WriteLine (Test.X);   // 0
class Test { public static int X; }   // Field
```

Default Values

All type instances have a default value. The default value for the predefined types is the result of a bitwise zeroing of memory and is null for reference types, 0 for numeric and enum types, '\0' for the char type, and false for the bool type.

You can obtain the default value for any type by using the `default` keyword (this is particularly useful with generics, as you'll see later). The default value in a custom value type (i.e., struct) is the same as the default value for each field defined by the custom type:

```
Console.WriteLine (default (decimal));    // 0
decimal d = default;
```

Parameters

A method can have a sequence of parameters. Parameters define the set of arguments that must be provided for that method. In this example, the method Foo has a single parameter named p, of type int:

```
Foo (8);                            // 8 is an argument
static void Foo (int p) {...}   // p is a parameter
```

You can control how parameters are passed with the ref, out, and in modifiers:

Parameter modifier	Passed by	Variable must be definitely assigned
None	Value	Going *in*
ref	Reference	Going *in*
in	Reference (read-only)	Going *in*
out	Reference	Going *out*

Passing arguments by value

By default, arguments in C# are *passed by value*, which is by far the most common case. This means that a copy of the value is created when it is passed to the method:

```
int x = 8;
Foo (x);                   // Make a copy of x
Console.WriteLine (x);   // x will still be 8

static void Foo (int p)
{
  p = p + 1;                 // Increment p by 1
  Console.WriteLine (p);   // Write p to screen
}
```

Assigning p a new value does not change the contents of x, because p and x reside in different memory locations.

Passing a reference type argument by value copies the *reference* but not the object. In the following example, Foo sees the same StringBuilder object we instantiated (sb) but has an independent *reference* to it. In other words, sb and fooSB are separate variables that reference the same StringBuilder object:

```
StringBuilder sb = new StringBuilder();
Foo (sb);
Console.WriteLine (sb.ToString());    // test

static void Foo (StringBuilder fooSB)
{
  fooSB.Append ("test");
  fooSB = null;
}
```

Because fooSB is a *copy* of a reference, setting it to null doesn't make sb null. (If, however, fooSB was declared and called with the ref modifier, sb *would* become null.)

The ref modifier

To *pass by reference*, C# provides the ref parameter modifier. In the following example, p and x refer to the same memory locations:

```
int x = 8;
Foo (ref  x);               // Ask Foo to deal
                            // directly with x
Console.WriteLine (x);      // x is now 9

static void Foo (ref int p)
{
  p = p + 1;                // Increment p by 1
  Console.WriteLine (p);    // Write p to screen
}
```

Now assigning p a new value changes the contents of x. Notice how the ref modifier is required both when writing and calling the method. This makes it very clear what's going on.

The out modifier

An `out` argument is like a `ref` argument, except for the following:

- It need not be assigned before going into the function.
- It must be assigned before it comes *out* of the function.

The `out` modifier is most commonly used to get multiple return values back from a method.

Out variables and discards

From C# 7, you can declare variables on the fly when calling methods with `out` parameters:

```
int.TryParse ("123", out int x);
Console.WriteLine (x);
```

This is equivalent to:

```
int x;
int.TryParse ("123", out x);
Console.WriteLine (x);
```

When calling methods with multiple `out` parameters, you can use an underscore to "discard" any in which you're uninterested. Assuming `SomeBigMethod` has been defined with five `out` parameters, you can ignore all but the third, as follows:

```
SomeBigMethod (out _, out _, out int x, out _, out _);
Console.WriteLine (x);
```

The in modifier

From C# 7.2, you can prefix a parameter with the in modifier to prevent it from being modified within the method. This allows the compiler to avoid the overhead of copying the argument prior to passing it in, which can matter in the case of large custom value types (see "Structs" on page 110).

The params modifier

The params modifier, if applied to the last parameter of a method, allows the method to accept any number of arguments of a particular type. The parameter type must be declared as a (single-dimensional) array. For example:

```
int Sum (params int[] ints)
{
  int sum = 0;
  for (int i = 0; i < ints.Length; i++) sum += ints[i];
  return sum;
}
```

You can call this as follows:

```
Console.WriteLine (Sum (1, 2, 3, 4));    // 10
```

If there are zero arguments in the params position, a zero-length array is created.

You can also supply a params argument as an ordinary array. The preceding call is semantically equivalent to:

```
Console.WriteLine (Sum (new int[] { 1, 2, 3, 4 } ));
```

Optional parameters

Methods, constructors, and indexers can declare *optional parameters*. A parameter is optional if it specifies a *default value* in its declaration:

```
void Foo (int x = 23) { Console.WriteLine (x); }
```

You can omit optional parameters when calling the method:

```
Foo();    // 23
```

The *default argument* of 23 is actually *passed* to the optional parameter x—the compiler bakes the value 23 into the compiled code at the *calling* side. The preceding call to Foo is semantically identical to

```
Foo (23);
```

because the compiler simply substitutes the default value of an optional parameter wherever it is used.

WARNING

Adding an optional parameter to a public method that's called from another assembly requires recompilation of both assemblies—just as though the parameter were mandatory.

The default value of an optional parameter must be specified by a constant expression, a parameterless constructor of a value type, or a `default` expression. You cannot mark optional parameters with `ref` or `out`.

Mandatory parameters must occur *before* optional parameters in both the method declaration and the method call (the exception is with `params` arguments, which still always come last). In the following example, the explicit value of 1 is passed to x, and the default value of 0 is passed to y:

```
Foo(1);    // 1, 0

void Foo (int x = 0, int y = 0)
{
  Console.WriteLine (x + ", " + y);
}
```

You can do the converse (pass a default value to x and an explicit value to y) by combining optional parameters with *named arguments*.

Named arguments

Rather than identifying an argument by position, you can identify an argument by name. For example:

```
Foo (x:1, y:2);  // 1, 2

void Foo (int x, int y)
{
  Console.WriteLine (x + ", " + y);
}
```

Named arguments can occur in any order. The following calls to Foo are semantically identical:

```
Foo (x:1, y:2);
Foo (y:2, x:1);
```

You can mix named and positional arguments, as long as the named arguments appear last:

```
Foo (1, y:2);
```

Named arguments are particularly useful in conjunction with optional parameters. For instance, consider the following method:

```
void Bar (int a=0, int b=0, int c=0, int d=0) { ... }
```

You can call this, supplying only a value for d, as follows:

```
Bar (d:3);
```

This is particularly useful when you're calling COM APIs.

var—Implicitly Typed Local Variables

It is often the case that you declare and initialize a variable in one step. If the compiler is able to infer the type from the initialization expression, you can use the word var in place of the type declaration. For example:

```
var x = "hello";
var y = new System.Text.StringBuilder();
var z = (float)Math.PI;
```

This is precisely equivalent to the following:

```
string x = "hello";
System.Text.StringBuilder y =
  new System.Text.StringBuilder();
float z = (float)Math.PI;
```

Because of this direct equivalence, implicitly typed variables are statically typed. For example, the following generates a compile-time error:

```
var x = 5;
x = "hello";    // Compile-time error; x is of type int
```

In the section "Anonymous Types" on page 176, we describe a scenario in which the use of var is mandatory.

Target-Typed new Expressions

Another way to reduce lexical repetition is with *target-typed new expressions* (from C# 9):

```
StringBuilder sb1 = new();
StringBuilder sb2 = new ("Test");
```

This is precisely equivalent to:

```
StringBuilder sb1 = new StringBuilder();
StringBuilder sb2 = new StringBuilder ("Test");
```

The principle is that you can call new without specifying a type name if the compiler is able to unambiguously infer it. Target-typed new expressions are particularly useful when the variable declaration and initialization are in different parts of your code. A common example is when you want to initialize a field in a constructor:

```
class Foo
{
  System.Text.StringBuilder sb;

  public Foo (string initialValue)
  {
    sb = new (initialValue);
  }
}
```

Target-typed new expressions are also helpful in the following scenario:

```
MyMethod (new ("test"));
void MyMethod (System.Text.StringBuilder sb) { ... }
```

Expressions and Operators

An *expression* essentially denotes a value. The simplest kinds of expressions are constants (such as 123) and variables (such as x). Expressions can be transformed and combined with operators. An *operator* takes one or more input *operands* to output a new expression:

```
12 * 30   // * is an operator; 12 and 30 are operands.
```

Complex expressions can be built because an operand can itself be an expression, such as the operand (12 * 30) in the following example:

```
1 + (12 * 30)
```

Operators in C# can be classed as *unary*, *binary*, or *ternary*, depending on the number of operands they work on (one, two, or three). The binary operators always use *infix* notation, in which the operator is placed *between* the two operands.

Operators that are intrinsic to the basic plumbing of the language are called *primary*; an example is the method call operator. An expression that has no value is called a *void expression*:

```
Console.WriteLine (1)
```

Because a void expression has no value, you cannot use it as an operand to build more complex expressions:

```
1 + Console.WriteLine (1)      // Compile-time error
```

Assignment Expressions

An *assignment expression* uses the = operator to assign the result of another expression to a variable. For example:

```
x = x * 5
```

An assignment expression is not a void expression. It actually carries the assignment value and so can be incorporated into another expression. In the following example, the expression assigns 2 to x and 10 to y:

```
y = 5 * (x = 2)
```

This style of expression can be used to initialize multiple values:

```
a = b = c = d = 0
```

The *compound assignment operators* are syntactic shortcuts that combine assignment with another operator. For example:

```
x *= 2     // equivalent to x = x * 2
x <<= 1    // equivalent to x = x << 1
```

(A subtle exception to this rule is with *events*, which we describe later: the += and -= operators here are treated specially and map to the event's add and remove accessors, respectively.)

Operator Precedence and Associativity

When an expression contains multiple operators, *precedence* and *associativity* determine the order of their evaluation. Operators with higher precedence execute before operators of lower precedence. If the operators have the same precedence, the operator's associativity determines the order of evaluation.

Precedence

The expression 1 + 2 * 3 is evaluated as 1 + (2 * 3) because * has a higher precedence than +.

Left-associative operators

Binary operators (except for assignment, lambda, and null-coalescing operators) are *left-associative*; in other words, they are evaluated from left to right. For example, the expression 8/4/2 is evaluated as (8/4)/2 due to left associativity. Of course, you can insert your own parentheses to change evaluation order.

Right-associative operators

The assignment and lambda operators, null-coalescing operator, and (ternary) conditional operator are *right-associative*; in other words, they are evaluated from right to left. Right associativity allows multiple assignments such as x=y=3 to compile: it works by first assigning 3 to y and then assigning the result of that expression (3) to x.

Operator Table

The following table lists C#'s operators in order of precedence. Operators listed under the same subheading have the same precedence. We explain user-overloadable operators in the section "Operator Overloading" on page 226.

Operator symbol	Operator name	Example	Overloadable
Primary (highest precedence)			
.	Member access	x.y	No
?.	Null-conditional	x?.y	No
! (postfix)	Null-forgiving	x!.y	No
->	Pointer to struct (unsafe)	x->y	No
()	Function call	x()	No
[]	Array/index	a[x]	Via indexer
++	Post-increment	x++	Yes
--	Post-decrement	x--	Yes
new	Create instance	new Foo()	No
stackalloc	Stack allocation	stackalloc(10)	No
typeof	Get type from identifier	typeof(int)	No
nameof	Get name of identifier	nameof(x)	No

Operator symbol	Operator name	Example	Overloadable
checked	Integral overflow check on	checked(x)	No
unchecked	Integral overflow check off	unchecked(x)	No
default	Default value	default(char)	No
sizeof	Get size of struct	sizeof(int)	No
Unary			
await	Await	await myTask	No
+	Positive value of	+x	Yes
-	Negative value of	-x	Yes
!	Not	!x	Yes
~	Bitwise complement	~x	Yes
++	Pre-increment	++x	Yes
--	Pre-decrement	--x	Yes
()	Cast	(int)x	No
^	Index from end	array[^1]	No
*	Value at address (unsafe)	*x	No
&	Address of value (unsafe)	&x	No
Range			
..	Range of indices	x..y	No
..^		x..^y	

Operator symbol	Operator name	Example	Overloadable
Switch and with			

switch	Switch expression	`num switch {`
		`  1 => true,`
		`  _ => false`
		`}`
			No

with	With expression	`rec with` `{ X = 123 }`	No
Multiplicative			
*	Multiply	`x * y`	Yes
/	Divide	`x / y`	Yes
%	Remainder	`x % y`	Yes
Additive			
+	Add	`x + y`	Yes
-	Subtract	`x - y`	Yes
Shift			
<<	Shift left	`x << 1`	Yes
>>	Shift right	`x >> 1`	Yes
>>>	Unsigned shift right	`x >>> 1`	Yes
Relational			
<	Less than	`x < y`	Yes
>	Greater than	`x > y`	Yes
<=	Less than or equal to	`x <= y`	Yes
>=	Greater than or equal to	`x >= y`	Yes
is	Type is or is subclass of	`x is y`	No

Operator symbol	Operator name	Example	Overloadable
as	Type conversion	x as y	No
Equality			
==	Equals	x == y	Yes
!=	Not equals	x != y	Yes
Bitwise And			
&	And	x & y	Yes
Bitwise Xor			
^	Exclusive Or	x ^ y	Yes
Bitwise Or			
|	Or	x | y	Yes
Conditional And			
&&	Conditional And	x && y	Via &
Conditional Or			
||	Conditional Or	x || y	Via |
Null coalescing			
??	Null coalescing	x ?? y	No
Conditional (Ternary)			
? :	Conditional	isTrue ? then This : elseThis	No
Assignment and lambda (lowest precedence)			
=	Assign	x = y	No
*=	Multiply self by	x *= 2	Via *
/=	Divide self by	x /= 2	Via /
+=	Add to self	x += 2	Via +
-=	Subtract from self	x -= 2	Via -

Operator symbol	Operator name	Example	Overloadable
<<=	Shift self left by	x <<= 2	Via <<
>>=	Shift self right by	x >>= 2	Via >>
>>>=	Unsigned shift self right by	x >>>= 2	Via >>>
&=	And self by	x &= 2	Via &
^=	Exclusive-Or self by	x ^= 2	Via ^
|=	Or self by	x |= 2	Via |
=>	Lambda	x => x + 1	No

Null Operators

C# provides three operators to make it easier to work with nulls: the *null-coalescing operator*, the *null-conditional operator*, and the *null-coalescing assignment operator*.

Null-Coalescing Operator

The ?? operator is the *null-coalescing operator*. It says, "If the operand to the left is non-null, give it to me; otherwise, give me another value." For example:

```
string s1 = null;
string s2 = s1 ?? "nothing"; // s2 evaluates to "nothing"
```

If the lefthand expression is non-null, the righthand expression is never evaluated. The null-coalescing operator also works with nullable value types (see "Nullable Value Types" on page 167).

Null-Coalescing Assignment Operator

The ??= operator (introduced in C# 8) is the *null-coalescing assignment operator*. It says, "If the operand to the left is null, assign the right operand to the left operand." Consider the following:

```
myVariable ??= someDefault;
```

This is equivalent to:

```
if (myVariable == null) myVariable = someDefault;
```

Null-Conditional Operator

The ?. operator is the *null-conditional* or "Elvis" operator. It allows you to call methods and access members just like the standard dot operator, except that if the operand on the left is null, the expression evaluates to null instead of throwing a NullReferenceException:

```
System.Text.StringBuilder sb = null;
string s = sb?.ToString();   // No error; s is null
```

The last line is equivalent to this:

```
string s = (sb == null ? null : sb.ToString());
```

Null-conditional expressions also work with indexers:

```
string[] words = null;
string word = words?[1];   // word is null
```

Upon encountering a null, the Elvis operator short-circuits the remainder of the expression. In the following example, s evaluates to null, even with a standard dot operator between ToString() and ToUpper():

```
System.Text.StringBuilder sb = null;
string s = sb?.ToString().ToUpper();   // No error
```

Repeated use of Elvis is necessary only if the operand immediately to its left might be null. The following expression is robust to both x being null and x.y being null:

```
x?.y?.z
```

This is equivalent to the following (except that x.y is evaluated only once):

```
x == null ? null
          : (x.y == null ? null : x.y.z)
```

The final expression must be capable of accepting a null. The following is illegal because int cannot accept a null:

```
System.Text.StringBuilder sb = null;
int length = sb?.ToString().Length;   // Illegal
```

We can fix this with the use of nullable value types (see "Nullable Value Types" on page 167):

```
int? length = sb?.ToString().Length;
// OK : int? can be null
```

You can also use the null-conditional operator to call a void method:

```
someObject?.SomeVoidMethod();
```

If someObject is null, this becomes a "no-operation" rather than throwing a NullReferenceException.

The null-conditional operator can be used with the commonly used type members that we describe in "Classes" on page 73, including *methods*, *fields*, *properties*, and *indexers*. It also combines well with the null-coalescing operator:

```
System.Text.StringBuilder sb = null;
string s = sb?.ToString() ?? "nothing";
// s evaluates to "nothing"
```

Statements

Functions comprise statements that execute sequentially in the textual order in which they appear. A *statement block* is a series of statements appearing between braces (the {} tokens).

Declaration Statements

A variable declaration introduces a new variable, optionally initializing it with an expression. You can declare multiple variables of the same type in a comma-separated list. For example:

```
bool rich = true, famous = false;
```

A constant declaration is like a variable declaration, except that it cannot be changed after it has been declared, and the initialization must occur with the declaration (more on this in "Constants" on page 74):

```
const double c = 2.99792458E08;
```

Local variable scope

The scope of a local variable or local constant variable extends throughout the current block. You cannot declare another local variable with the same name in the current block or in any nested blocks.

Expression Statements

Expression statements are expressions that are also valid statements. In practice, this means expressions that "do" something; in other words:

- Assign or modify a variable
- Instantiate an object
- Call a method

Expressions that do none of these are not valid statements:

```
string s = "foo";
s.Length;              // Illegal statement: does nothing!
```

When you call a constructor or a method that returns a value, you're not obliged to use the result. However, unless the constructor or method changes state, the statement is useless:

```
new StringBuilder();    // Legal, but useless
x.Equals (y);           // Legal, but useless
```

Selection Statements

Selection statements conditionally control the flow of program execution.

The if statement

An if statement executes a statement if a bool expression is true. For example:

```
if (5 < 2 * 3)
  Console.WriteLine ("true");        // true
```

The statement can be a code block:

```
if (5 < 2 * 3)
{
  Console.WriteLine ("true");        // true
  Console.WriteLine ("...")
}
```

The else clause

An if statement can optionally feature an else clause:

```
if (2 + 2 == 5)
  Console.WriteLine ("Does not compute");
else
  Console.WriteLine ("False");       // False
```

Within an else clause, you can nest another if statement:

```
if (2 + 2 == 5)
  Console.WriteLine ("Does not compute");
else
  if (2 + 2 == 4)
    Console.WriteLine ("Computes");    // Computes
```

Changing the flow of execution with braces

An else clause always applies to the immediately preceding if statement in the statement block. For example:

```
if (true)
  if (false)
    Console.WriteLine();
  else
    Console.WriteLine ("executes");
```

This is semantically identical to the following:

```
if (true)
{
```

```
    if (false)
      Console.WriteLine();
    else
      Console.WriteLine ("executes");
}
```

You can change the execution flow by moving the braces:

```
if (true)
{
  if (false)
    Console.WriteLine();
}
else
  Console.WriteLine ("does not execute");
```

C# has no "elseif" keyword; however, the following pattern achieves the same result:

```
if (age >= 35)
  Console.WriteLine ("You can be president!");
else if (age >= 21)
  Console.WriteLine ("You can drink!");
else if (age >= 18)
  Console.WriteLine ("You can vote!");
else
  Console.WriteLine ("You can wait!");
```

The switch statement

Switch statements let you branch program execution based on a selection of possible values that a variable might have. Switch statements can result in cleaner code than multiple if statements because switch statements require an expression to be evaluated only once. For instance:

```
static void ShowCard (int cardNumber)
{
  switch (cardNumber)
  {
    case 13:
      Console.WriteLine ("King");
      break;
    case 12:
      Console.WriteLine ("Queen");
      break;
```

```
      case 11:
        Console.WriteLine ("Jack");
        break;
      default:      // Any other cardNumber
        Console.WriteLine (cardNumber);
        break;
  }
}
```

The values in each case expression must be constants, which restricts their allowable types to the built-in numeric types and the bool, char, string, and enum types. At the end of each case clause, you must say explicitly where execution is to go next with some kind of jump statement. Here are the options:

- break (jumps to the end of the switch statement)
- goto case *x* (jumps to another case clause)
- goto default (jumps to the default clause)
- Any other jump statement—namely, return, throw, continue, or goto *label*

When more than one value should execute the same code, you can list the common cases sequentially:

```
switch (cardNumber)
{
  case 13:
  case 12:
  case 11:
    Console.WriteLine ("Face card");
    break;
  default:
    Console.WriteLine ("Plain card");
    break;
}
```

This feature of a switch statement can be pivotal in terms of producing cleaner code than multiple if-else statements.

Switching on types

From C# 7, you can switch on *type*:

```
static void TellMeTheType (object x)
{
  switch (x)
  {
    case int i:
      Console.WriteLine ("It's an int!");
      break;
    case string s:
      Console.WriteLine (s.Length);        // We can use s
      break;
    case bool b when b == true:   // Fires when b is true
      Console.WriteLine ("True");
      break;
    case null:     // You can also switch on null
      Console.WriteLine ("null");
      break;
  }
}
```

(The object type allows for a variable of any type—see "Inheritance" on page 95 and "The object Type" on page 106.)

Each *case* clause specifies a type upon which to match, and a variable upon which to assign the typed value if the match succeeds. Unlike with constants, there's no restriction on what types you can use. The optional when clause specifies a condition that must be satisfied for the case to match.

The order of the case clauses is relevant when you're switching on type (unlike when you're switching on constants). An exception to this rule is the default clause, which is executed last, regardless of where it appears.

You can stack multiple case clauses. The Console.WriteLine in the following code will execute for any floating-point type greater than 1,000:

```
switch (x)
{
  case float f when f > 1000:
  case double d when d > 1000:
  case decimal m when m > 1000:
    Console.WriteLine ("f, d and m are out of scope");
    break;
```

In this example, the compiler lets us consume the variables f, d, and m, *only* in the when clauses. When we call Console.Write Line, it's unknown as to which one of those three variables will be assigned, so the compiler puts all of them out of scope.

Switch expressions

From C# 8, you can also use switch in the context of an *expression*. Assuming cardNumber is of type int, the following illustrates its use:

```
string cardName = cardNumber switch
{
  13 => "King",
  12 => "Queen",
  11 => "Jack",
  _ => "Pip card"    // equivalent to 'default'
};
```

Notice that the switch keyword appears *after* the variable name and that the case clauses are expressions (terminated by commas) rather than statements. You can also switch on multiple values (*tuples*):

```
int cardNumber = 12; string suite = "spades";
string cardName = (cardNumber, suite) switch
{
  (13, "spades") => "King of spades",
  (13, "clubs") => "King of clubs",
  ...
};
```

Iteration Statements

C# enables a sequence of statements to execute repeatedly with the while, do-while, for, and foreach statements.

while and do-while loops

while loops repeatedly execute a body of code while a bool expression is true. The expression is tested *before* the body of the loop is executed. For example, the following writes 012:

```
int i = 0;
while (i < 3)
{                          // Braces here are optional
  Console.Write (i++);
}
```

do-while loops differ in functionality from while loops only in that they test the expression *after* the statement block has executed (ensuring that the block is always executed at least once). Here's the preceding example rewritten with a do-while loop:

```
int i = 0;
do
{
  Console.WriteLine (i++);
}
while (i < 3);
```

for loops

for loops are like while loops with special clauses for *initialization* and *iteration* of a loop variable. A for loop contains three clauses as follows:

```
for (init-clause; condition-clause; iteration-clause)
  statement-or-statement-block
```

The *init-clause* executes before the loop begins and typically initializes one or more *iteration* variables.

The *condition-clause* is a bool expression that is tested *before* each loop iteration. The body executes while this condition is true.

The *iteration-clause* is executed *after* each iteration of the body. It's typically used to update the iteration variable.

For example, the following prints the numbers 0 through 2:

```
for (int i = 0; i < 3; i++)
  Console.WriteLine (i);
```

The following prints the first 10 Fibonacci numbers (where each number is the sum of the previous two):

```
for (int i = 0, prevFib = 1, curFib = 1; i < 10; i++)
{
  Console.WriteLine (prevFib);
  int newFib = prevFib + curFib;
  prevFib = curFib; curFib = newFib;
}
```

Any of the three parts of the for statement can be omitted. You can implement an infinite loop such as the following (though while(true) can be used instead):

```
for (;;) Console.WriteLine ("interrupt me");
```

foreach loops

The foreach statement iterates over each element in an enumerable object. Most of the .NET types that represent a set or list of elements are enumerable. For example, both an array and a string are enumerable. Here is an example of enumerating over the characters in a string, from the first character through the last:

```
foreach (char c in "beer")
  Console.Write (c + " ");   // b e e r
```

We define enumerable objects in "Enumeration and Iterators" on page 161.

Jump Statements

The C# jump statements are break, continue, goto, return, and throw. We cover the throw keyword in "try Statements and Exceptions" on page 153.

The break statement

The break statement ends the execution of the body of an iteration or switch statement:

```
int x = 0;
while (true)
{
  if (x++ > 5) break;        // break from the loop
}
```

```
// execution continues here after break
...
```

The continue statement

The continue statement forgoes the remaining statements in the loop and makes an early start on the next iteration. The following loop *skips* even numbers:

```
for (int i = 0; i < 10; i++)
{
  if ((i % 2) == 0) continue;
  Console.Write (i + " ");      // 1 3 5 7 9
}
```

The goto statement

The goto statement transfers execution to a label (denoted with a colon suffix) within a statement block. The following iterates the numbers 1 through 5, mimicking a for loop:

```
int i = 1;
startLoop:
if (i <= 5)
{
  Console.Write (i + " ");   // 1 2 3 4 5
  i++;
  goto startLoop;
}
```

The return statement

The return statement exits the method and must return an expression of the method's return type if the method is non-void:

```
decimal AsPercentage (decimal d)
{
  decimal p = d * 100m;
  return p;      // Return to calling method with value
}
```

A return statement can appear anywhere in a method (except in a finally block) and can be used more than once.

Namespaces

A *namespace* is a domain within which type names must be unique. Types are typically organized into hierarchical namespaces—both to avoid naming conflicts and to make type names easier to find. For example, the RSA type that handles public key encryption is defined within the following namespace:

```
System.Security.Cryptography
```

A namespace forms an integral part of a type's name. The following code calls RSA's Create method:

```
System.Security.Cryptography.RSA rsa =
  System.Security.Cryptography.RSA.Create();
```

NOTE

Namespaces are independent of assemblies, which are units of deployment such as an *.exe* or *.dll*.

Namespaces also have no impact on member accessibility —public, internal, private, and so on.

The namespace keyword defines a namespace for types within that block. For example:

```
namespace Outer.Middle.Inner
{
  class Class1 {}
  class Class2 {}
}
```

The dots in the namespace indicate a hierarchy of nested namespaces. The code that follows is semantically identical to the preceding example:

```
namespace Outer
{
  namespace Middle
  {
```

```
  namespace Inner
  {
    class Class1 {}
    class Class2 {}
  }
 }
}
```

You can refer to a type with its *fully qualified name*, which includes all namespaces from the outermost to the innermost. For example, you could refer to Class1 in the preceding example as Outer.Middle.Inner.Class1.

Types not defined in any namespace are said to reside in the *global namespace*. The global namespace also includes top-level namespaces, such as Outer in our example.

File-Scoped Namespaces

Often, you will want all the types in a file to be defined in one namespace:

```
namespace MyNamespace
{
  class Class1 {}
  class Class2 {}
}
```

From C# 10, you can accomplish this with a *file-scoped namespace*:

```
namespace MyNamespace;   // Applies to everything below

class Class1 {}          // inside MyNamespace
class Class2 {}          // inside MyNamespace
```

File-scoped namespaces reduce clutter and eliminate an unnecessary level of indentation.

The using Directive

The using directive *imports* a namespace and is a convenient way to refer to types without their fully qualified names. For example, you can refer to Class1 in the preceding example as follows:

```
using Outer.Middle.Inner;

Class1 c;    // Don't need fully qualified name
```

A using directive can be nested within a namespace itself to limit the scope of the directive.

The global using Directive

From C# 10, if you prefix a using directive with the global keyword, the directive will apply to all files in the project or compilation unit:

```
global using System;
global using System.Collection.Generic;
```

This lets you centralize common imports and avoid repeating the same directives in every file.

global using directives must precede nonglobal directives and cannot appear inside namespace declarations. The global directive can be used with using static.

using static

The using static directive imports a *type* rather than a namespace. All static members of that type can then be used without being qualified with the type name. In the following example, we call the Console class's static WriteLine method:

```
using static System.Console;

WriteLine ("Hello");
```

The using static directive imports all accessible static members of the type, including fields, properties, and nested types. You can also apply this directive to enum types (see "Enums" on page 121), in which case their members are imported. Should an ambiguity arise between multiple static imports, the

C# compiler is unable to infer the correct type from the context and will generate an error.

Rules Within a Namespace

Name scoping

Names declared in outer namespaces can be used unqualified within inner namespaces. In this example, Class1 does not need qualification within Inner:

```
namespace Outer
{
  class Class1 {}

  namespace Inner
  {
    class Class2 : Class1 {}
  }
}
```

If you want to refer to a type in a different branch of your namespace hierarchy, you can use a partially qualified name. In the following example, we base SalesReport on Common.Report Base:

```
namespace MyTradingCompany
{
  namespace Common
  {
    class ReportBase {}
  }
  namespace ManagementReporting
  {
    class SalesReport : Common.ReportBase {}
  }
}
```

Name hiding

If the same type name appears in both an inner and an outer namespace, the inner name wins. To refer to the type in the outer namespace, you must qualify its name.

Repeated namespaces

You can repeat a namespace declaration, as long as the type names within the namespaces don't conflict:

```
namespace Outer.Middle.Inner { class Class1 {} }
namespace Outer.Middle.Inner { class Class2 {} }
```

The classes can even span source files and assemblies.

The global:: qualifier

Occasionally, a fully qualified type name might conflict with an inner name. You can force C# to use the fully qualified type name by prefixing it with global::, as follows:

```
global::System.Text.StringBuilder sb;
```

Aliasing Types and Namespaces

Importing a namespace can result in type-name collision. Rather than importing the whole namespace, you can import just the specific types you need, giving each type an alias. For example:

```
using PropertyInfo2 = System.Reflection.PropertyInfo;
class Program { PropertyInfo2 p; }
```

An entire namespace can be aliased, as follows:

```
using R = System.Reflection;
class Program { R.PropertyInfo p; }
```

Alias any type (C# 12)

From C# 12, the using directive can alias any kind of type, including, for instance, arrays:

```
using NumberList = double[];
NumberList numbers = { 2.5, 3.5 };
```

You can also alias tuples (see "Tuples" on page 177).

Classes

A *class* is the most common kind of reference type. The simplest possible class declaration is as follows:

```
class Foo
{
}
```

A more complex class optionally has the following:

Preceding the keyword class	*Attributes* and *class modifiers*. The non-nested class modifiers are public, internal, abstract, sealed, static, unsafe, and partial.
Following Foo	*Generic type parameters* and *constraints*, a *base class*, and *interfaces*.
Within the braces	*Class members* (these are *methods*, *properties*, *indexers*, *events*, *fields*, *constructors*, *overloaded operators*, *nested types*, and a *finalizer*).

Fields

A *field* is a variable that is a member of a class or struct. For example:

```
class Octopus
{
  string name;
  public int Age = 10;
}
```

A field can have the readonly modifier to prevent it from being modified after construction. A read-only field can be assigned only in its declaration or within the enclosing type's constructor.

Field initialization is optional. An uninitialized field has a default value (0, '\0', null, false). Field initializers run before constructors in the order in which they appear.

For convenience, you can declare multiple fields of the same type in a comma-separated list. This is a convenient way for all the fields to share the same attributes and field modifiers. For example:

```
static readonly int legs = 8, eyes = 2;
```

Constants

A *constant* is evaluated statically at compile time, and the compiler literally substitutes its value whenever used (rather like a macro in C++). A constant can be any of the built-in numeric types: bool, char, string, or an enum type.

A constant is declared with the const keyword and must be initialized with a value. For example:

```
public class Test
{
  public const string Message = "Hello World";
}
```

A constant is much more restrictive than a static readonly field—both in the types you can use and in field initialization semantics. A constant also differs from a static readonly field in that the evaluation of the constant occurs at compile time. Constants can also be declared local to a method:

```
static void Main()
{
  const double twoPI = 2 * System.Math.PI;
  ...
}
```

Methods

A *method* performs an action in a series of statements. A method can receive *input* data from the caller by specifying *parameters* and send *output* data back to the caller by specifying a *return type*. A method can specify a void return type, indicating that it doesn't return any value to its caller. A method can also output data back to the caller via ref and out parameters.

A method's *signature* must be unique within the type. A method's signature comprises its name and parameter types in order (but not the parameter *names* nor the return type).

Expression-bodied methods

A method that comprises a single expression, such as the following:

```
int Foo (int x) { return x * 2; }
```

can be written more tersely as an *expression-bodied method*. A fat arrow replaces the braces and return keyword:

```
int Foo (int x) => x * 2;
```

Expression-bodied functions can also have a void return type:

```
void Foo (int x) => Console.WriteLine (x);
```

Local methods

You can define a method within another method:

```
void WriteCubes()
{
  Console.WriteLine (Cube (3));

  int Cube (int value) => value * value * value;
}
```

The local method (Cube, in this case) is visible only to the enclosing method (WriteCubes). This simplifies the containing type and instantly signals to anyone looking at the code that Cube is used nowhere else. Local methods can access the local variables and parameters of the enclosing method. This has a number of consequences, which we describe in "Capturing Outer Variables" on page 149.

Local methods can appear within other function kinds, such as property accessors, constructors, and so on, and even within other local methods. Local methods can be iterators or asynchronous.

Methods declared in top-level statements are implicitly local; we can demonstrate this as follows:

```
int x = 3; Foo();
void Foo() => Console.WriteLine (x);  // We can access x
```

Static local methods

Adding the static modifier to a local method (from C# 8) prevents it from seeing the local variables and parameters of the enclosing method. This helps to reduce coupling and prevents the local method from accidentally referring to variables in the containing method.

Overloading methods

WARNING

Local methods cannot be overloaded. This means that methods declared in top-level statements (which are treated as local methods) cannot be overloaded.

A type can overload methods (have multiple methods with the same name) as long as the parameter types are different. For example, the following methods can all coexist in the same type:

```
void Foo (int x);
void Foo (double x);
void Foo (int x, float y);
void Foo (float x, int y);
```

Instance Constructors

Constructors run initialization code on a class or struct. A constructor is defined like a method, except that the method

---

name and return type are reduced to the name of the enclosing type:

```
Panda p = new Panda ("Petey");   // Call constructor

public class Panda
{
  string name;              // Define field
  public Panda (string n)   // Define constructor
  {
    name = n;               // Initialization code
  }
}
```

Single-statement constructors can be written as expression-bodied members:

```
public Panda (string n) => name = n;
```

A class or struct can overload constructors. One overload can call another, using the this keyword:

```
public class Wine
{
  public Wine (decimal price) {...}

  public Wine (decimal price, int year)
    : this (price) {...}
}
```

When one constructor calls another, the *called constructor* executes first.

You can pass an *expression* into another constructor as follows:

```
public Wine (decimal price, DateTime year)
  : this (price, year.Year) {...}
```

The expression itself cannot make use of the this reference, for example, to call an instance method. It can, however, call static methods.

Implicit parameterless constructors

For classes, the C# compiler automatically generates a parameterless public constructor if and only if you do not define any constructors. However, as soon as you define at least one constructor, the parameterless constructor is no longer automatically generated.

Nonpublic constructors

Constructors do not need to be public. A common reason to have a nonpublic constructor is to control instance creation via a static method call. The static method could be used to return an object from a pool rather than creating a new object or to return a specialized subclass chosen based on input arguments.

Deconstructors

Whereas a constructor typically takes a set of values (as parameters) and assigns them to fields, a deconstructor (C# 7+) does the reverse and assigns fields back to a set of variables. A deconstruction method must be called Deconstruct and have one or more out parameters:

```
class Rectangle
{
  public readonly float Width, Height;

  public Rectangle (float width, float height)
  {
    Width = width; Height = height;
  }

  public void Deconstruct (out float width,
                           out float height)
  {
    width = Width; height = Height;
  }
}
```

To call the deconstructor, you use the following special syntax:

```
var rect = new Rectangle (3, 4);
(float width, float height) = rect;
Console.WriteLine (width + " " + height);    // 3 4
```

The second line is the deconstructing call. It creates two local variables and then calls the `Deconstruct` method. Our deconstructing call is equivalent to the following:

```
rect.Deconstruct (out var width, out var height);
```

Deconstructing calls allow implicit typing, so we could shorten our call to:

```
(var width, var height) = rect;
```

Or simply:

```
var (width, height) = rect;
```

If the variables into which you're deconstructing are already defined, omit the types altogether; this is called a *deconstructing assignment*:

```
(width, height) = rect;
```

You can offer the caller a range of deconstruction options by overloading the `Deconstruct` method.

NOTE

The `Deconstruct` method can be an extension method (see "Extension Methods" on page 174). This is a useful trick if you want to deconstruct types that you did not author.

From C# 10, you can mix and match existing and new variables when deconstructing:

```
double x1 = 0;
(x1, double y2) = rect;
```

Object Initializers

To simplify object initialization, the accessible fields or properties of an object can be initialized via an *object initializer* directly after construction. For example, consider the following class:

```csharp
public class Bunny
{
  public string Name;
  public bool LikesCarrots, LikesHumans;

  public Bunny () {}
  public Bunny (string n) => Name = n;
}
```

Using object initializers, you can instantiate Bunny objects as follows:

```csharp
Bunny b1 = new Bunny {
                       Name="Bo",
                       LikesCarrots = true,
                       LikesHumans = false
                     };

Bunny b2 = new Bunny ("Bo") {
                             LikesCarrots = true,
                             LikesHumans = false
                           };
```

The this Reference

The this reference refers to the instance itself. In the following example, the Marry method uses this to set the partner's mate field:

```csharp
public class Panda
{
  public Panda Mate;

  public void Marry (Panda partner)
  {
    Mate = partner;
    partner.Mate = this;
```

```
    }
  }
```

The `this` reference also disambiguates a local variable or parameter from a field. For example:

```
public class Test
{
  string name;
  public Test (string name) => this.name = name;
}
```

The `this` reference is valid only within nonstatic members of a class or struct.

Properties

Properties look like fields from the outside, but internally they contain logic, like methods do. For example, you can't determine by looking at the following code whether `CurrentPrice` is a field or a property:

```
Stock msft = new Stock();
msft.CurrentPrice = 30;
msft.CurrentPrice -= 3;
Console.WriteLine (msft.CurrentPrice);
```

A property is declared like a field but with a `get`/`set` block added. Here's how to implement `CurrentPrice` as a property:

```
public class Stock
{
  decimal currentPrice;   // The private "backing" field

  public decimal CurrentPrice     // The public property
  {
    get { return currentPrice; }
    set { currentPrice = value; }
  }
}
```

`get` and `set` denote property *accessors*. The `get` accessor runs when the property is read. It must return a value of the property's type. The `set` accessor runs when the property is assigned. It has an implicit parameter named `value` of the property's type that you typically assign to a private field (in this case, currentPrice).

Although properties are accessed in the same way as fields, they differ in that they give the implementer complete control over getting and setting its value. This control enables the implementer to choose whatever internal representation is needed, without exposing the internal details to the user of the property. In this example, the set method could throw an exception if value was outside a valid range of values.

NOTE

Throughout this book, we use public fields to keep the examples free of distraction. In a real application, you would typically favor public properties over public fields to promote encapsulation.

A property is read-only if it specifies only a get accessor, and it is write-only if it specifies only a set accessor. Write-only properties are rarely used.

A property typically has a dedicated backing field to store the underlying data. However, it doesn't need to; it can instead return a value computed from other data:

```
decimal currentPrice, sharesOwned;

public decimal Worth
{
  get { return currentPrice * sharesOwned; }
}
```

Expression-bodied properties

You can declare a read-only property, such as the preceding one, more tersely as an *expression-bodied property*. A fat arrow replaces all the braces and the get and return keywords:

```
public decimal Worth => currentPrice * sharesOwned;
```

From C# 7, set accessors can be expression-bodied too:

```
public decimal Worth
{
  get => currentPrice * sharesOwned;
  set => sharesOwned = value / currentPrice;
}
```

Automatic properties

The most common implementation for a property is a getter and/or setter that simply reads and writes to a private field of the same type as the property. An *automatic property* declaration instructs the compiler to provide this implementation. We can improve the first example in this section by declaring CurrentPrice as an automatic property:

```
public class Stock
{
  public decimal CurrentPrice { get; set; }
}
```

The compiler automatically generates a private backing field of a compiler-generated name that cannot be referred to. The set accessor can be marked private or protected if you want to expose the property as read-only to other types.

Property initializers

You can add a *property initializer* to automatic properties, just as with fields:

```
public decimal CurrentPrice { get; set; } = 123;
```

This gives CurrentPrice an initial value of 123. Properties with an initializer can be read-only:

```
public int Maximum { get; } = 999;
```

Just as with read-only fields, read-only automatic properties can also be assigned in the type's constructor. This is useful in creating *immutable* (read-only) types.

get and set accessibility

The get and set accessors can have different access levels. The typical use case for this is to have a public property with an internal or private access modifier on the setter:

```
private decimal x;
public decimal X
{
  get        { return x;  }
  private set { x = Math.Round (value, 2); }
}
```

Notice that you declare the property itself with the more permissive access level (public, in this case) and add the modifier to the accessor you want to be *less* accessible.

Init-only setters

From C# 9, you can declare a property accessor with init instead of set:

```
public class Note
{
  public int Pitch    { get; init; } = 20;
  public int Duration { get; init; } = 100;
}
```

These *init-only* properties act like read-only properties, except that they can also be set via an object initializer:

```
var note = new Note { Pitch = 50 };
```

After that, the property cannot be altered:

```
note.Pitch = 200;  // Error - init-only setter!
```

Init-only properties cannot even be set from inside their class, except via their property initializer, the constructor, or another init-only accessor.

The alternative to init-only properties is to have read-only properties that you populate via a constructor:

```
public Note (int pitch = 20, int duration = 100)
{
  Pitch = pitch; Duration = duration;
}
```

Should the class be part of a public library, this approach makes versioning difficult, in that adding an optional parameter to the constructor at a later date breaks binary compatibility with consumers (whereas adding a new init-only property breaks nothing).

NOTE

Init-only properties have another significant advantage, which is that they allow for nondestructive mutation when used in conjunction with records (see "Records" on page 179).

Just as with ordinary set accessors, init-only accessors can provide an implementation:

```
public class Point
{
  readonly int _x;
  public int X { get => _x; init => _x = value; }
  ...
```

Notice that the _x field is read-only: init-only setters are permitted to modify readonly fields in their own class. (Without this feature, _x would need to be writable, and the class would fail at being internally immutable.)

Indexers

Indexers provide a natural syntax for accessing elements in a class or struct that encapsulate a list or dictionary of values. Indexers are similar to properties but are accessed via an index argument rather than a property name. The string class has an indexer that lets you access each of its char values via an int index:

```
string s = "hello";
Console.WriteLine (s[0]); // 'h'
Console.WriteLine (s[3]); // 'l'
```

The syntax for using indexers is like that for using arrays, except that the index argument(s) can be of any type(s). You can call indexers null-conditionally by inserting a question mark before the square bracket (see "Null Operators" on page 56):

```
string s = null;
Console.WriteLine (s?[0]);  // Writes nothing; no error.
```

Implementing an indexer

To write an indexer, define a property called this, specifying the arguments in square brackets. For example:

```
class Sentence
{
  string[] words = "The quick brown fox".Split();

  public string this [int wordNum]      // indexer
  {
    get { return words [wordNum];  }
    set { words [wordNum] = value; }
  }
}
```

Here's how we could use this indexer:

```
Sentence s = new Sentence();
Console.WriteLine (s[3]);        // fox
s[3] = "kangaroo";
Console.WriteLine (s[3]);        // kangaroo
```

A type can declare multiple indexers, each with parameters of different types. An indexer can also take more than one parameter:

```
public string this [int arg1, string arg2]
{
```

```
  get { ... }  set { ... }
}
```

If you omit the set accessor, an indexer becomes read-only, and expression-bodied syntax can be used to shorten its definition:

```
public string this [int wordNum] => words [wordNum];
```

Using indices and ranges with indexers

You can support indices and ranges (see "Indices and Ranges" on page 36) in your own classes by defining an indexer with a parameter type of Index or Range. We could extend our previous example by adding the following indexers to the Sentence class:

```
public string this [Index index] => words [index];
public string[] this [Range range] => words [range];
```

This then enables the following:

```
Sentence s = new Sentence();
Console.WriteLine (s [^1]);        // fox
string[] firstTwoWords = s [..2];   // (The, quick)
```

Primary Constructors (C# 12)

From C# 12, you can include a parameter list directly after a class (or struct) declaration:

```
class Person (string firstName, string lastName)
{
  public void Print() =>
    Console.WriteLine (firstName + " " + lastName);
}
```

This instructs the compiler to automatically build a *primary constructor* using the *primary constructor parameters* (first Name and lastName) so that we can instantiate our class as follows:

```
Person p = new Person ("Alice", "Jones");
p.Print();    // Alice Jones
```

Primary constructors are useful for prototyping and other simple scenarios. The alternative would be to define fields to store firstName and lastName and then write a constructor to populate them.

The constructor that C# builds is called primary because any additional constructors that you choose to (explicitly) write must invoke it:

```
class Person (string firstName, string lastName)
{
  public Person (string first, string last, int age)
    : this (first, last)  // Must call primary constructor
  { ... }
}
```

This ensures that primary constructor parameters are *always populated*.

NOTE

C# also provides *records*, which we cover in "Records" on page 179. Records also support primary constructors; however, the compiler takes an extra step with records and generates (by default) a public init-only property for each primary constructor parameter.

Primary constructors are best suited to simple scenarios due to the following limitations:

- You cannot add extra initialization code to a primary constructor.
- Although it's easy to expose a primary constructor parameter as a public property, you cannot easily incorporate validation logic unless the property is read-only.

Primary constructors displace the default parameterless constructor that C# would otherwise generate.

Primary constructor semantics

To understand how primary constructors work, consider how an ordinary constructor behaves:

```
class Person
{
  public Person (string firstName, string lastName)
  {
    ... do something with firstName, lastName
  }
}
```

When the code inside this constructor finishes executing, parameters `firstName` and `lastName` disappear out of scope and cannot be subsequently accessed. In contrast, a primary constructor's parameters do *not* disappear out of scope and can be subsequently accessed from anywhere within the class, for the life of the object.

NOTE

Primary constructor parameters are special C# constructs, not *fields*, although the compiler does end up generating hidden fields behind the scenes to store their values if necessary.

Primary constructors and field/property initializers

The accessibility of primary constructor parameters extends to field and property initializers. In the following example, we use field and property initializers to assign `firstName` to a public field and `lastName` to a public property:

```
class Person (string firstName, string lastName)
{
  public readonly string FirstName = firstName;
  public string LastName { get; } = lastName;
}
```

Masking primary constructor parameters

Fields (or properties) can reuse primary constructor parameter names:

```
class Person (string firstName, string lastName)
{
  readonly string firstName = firstName;
  readonly string lastName = lastName;
}
```

In this scenario, the field or property takes precedence, thereby masking the primary constructor parameter, *except* on the righthand side of field and property initializers (shown in boldface).

NOTE

Just like ordinary parameters, primary constructor parameters are writable. Masking them with a same-named `readonly` field (as in our example) effectively protects them from subsequent modification.

Validating primary constructor parameters

In "throw expressions" on page 159, we will describe how to throw exceptions when encountering scenarios such as invalid data. Here's a preview to illustrate how this can be used with primary constructors to validate `lastName` upon construction, ensuring that it cannot be null:

```
new Person ("Alice", null);   // throws exception

class Person (string firstName, string lastName)
{
  readonly string lastName = (lastName == null)
    ? throw new ArgumentNullException ("lastName")
    : lastName;
}
```

(Remember that code within a field or property initializer executes when the object is constructed—not when the field or property is accessed.) The same technique can also expose lastName as a public read-only property:

```
public string LastName { get; } = (lastName == null)
  ? throw new ArgumentNullException ("lastName")
  : lastName;
```

Static Constructors

A static constructor executes once per *type*, rather than once per *instance*. A type can define only one static constructor, and it must be parameterless and have the same name as the type:

```
class Test
{
  static Test() { Console.Write ("Type Initialized"); }
}
```

The runtime automatically invokes a static constructor just prior to the type being used. Two things trigger this: instantiating the type and accessing a static member in the type.

WARNING

If a static constructor throws an unhandled exception, that type becomes *unusable* for the life of the application.

Static field initializers run just *before* the static constructor is called. If a type has no static constructor, static field initializers will execute just prior to the type being used—or *anytime earlier* at the whim of the runtime.

Static Classes

A class marked as static cannot be instantiated or subclassed, and must be composed solely of static members. The System.Console and System.Math classes are good examples of static classes.

Finalizers

Finalizers are class-only methods that execute before the garbage collector reclaims the memory for an unreferenced object. The syntax for a finalizer is the name of the class prefixed with the ~ symbol:

```
class Class1
{
  ~Class1() { ... }
}
```

C# translates a finalizer into a method that overrides the Finalize method in the object class. We discuss garbage collection and finalizers fully in Chapter 12 of *C# 12 in a Nutshell*.

Single-statement finalizers can be written with expression-bodied syntax.

Partial Types and Methods

Partial types allow a type definition to be split—typically across multiple files. A common scenario is for a partial class to be autogenerated from some other source (e.g., a Visual Studio template) and for that class to be augmented with additional hand-authored methods. For example:

```
// PaymentFormGen.cs - autogenerated
partial class PaymentForm { ... }

// PaymentForm.cs - hand-authored
partial class PaymentForm { ... }
```

Each participant must have the `partial` declaration.

Participants cannot have conflicting members. A constructor with the same parameters, for instance, cannot be repeated. Partial types are resolved entirely by the compiler, which means that each participant must be available at compile time and must reside in the same assembly.

A base class can be specified on a single participant or on multiple participants (as long as the base class that you specify is the same). In addition, each participant can independently specify interfaces to implement. We cover base classes and interfaces in "Inheritance" on page 95 and "Interfaces" on page 115.

Partial methods

A partial type can contain *partial methods*. These let an auto-generated partial type provide customizable hooks for manual authoring. For example:

```
partial class PaymentForm     // In autogenerated file
{
  partial void ValidatePayment (decimal amount);
}
```

```
partial class PaymentForm     // In hand-authored file
{
  partial void ValidatePayment (decimal amount)
  {
    if (amount > 100) Console.Write ("Expensive!");
  }
}
```

A partial method consists of two parts: a *definition* and an *implementation*. The definition is typically written by a code generator, and the implementation is typically manually authored. If an implementation is not provided, the definition of the partial method is compiled away (as is the code that calls it). This allows autogenerated code to be liberal in providing hooks, without having to worry about bloat. Partial methods must be void and are implicitly private.

Extended partial methods

Extended partial methods (from C# 9) are designed for the reverse code generation scenario, where a programmer defines hooks that a code generator implements. An example of where this might occur is with *source generators*, a Roslyn feature that lets you feed the compiler an assembly that automatically generates portions of your code.

A partial method declaration is *extended* if it begins with an accessibility modifier:

```
public partial class Test
{
  public partial void M1();   // Extended partial method
  private partial void M2();  // Extended partial method
}
```

The presence of the accessibility modifier doesn't just affect accessibility: it tells the compiler to treat the declaration differently.

Extended partial methods *must* have implementations; they do not melt away if unimplemented. In this example, both M1 and M2 must have implementations because they each specify accessibility modifiers (public and private).

Because they cannot melt away, extended partial methods can return any type and can include out parameters.

The nameof Operator

The nameof operator returns the name of any symbol (type, member, variable, and so on) as a string:

```
int count = 123;
string name = nameof (count);        // name is "count"
```

Its advantage over simply specifying a string is that of static type checking. Tools such as Visual Studio can understand the symbol reference, so if you rename the symbol in question, all of its references will be renamed too.

To specify the name of a type member such as a field or property, include the type as well. This works with both static and instance members:

```
string name = nameof (StringBuilder.Length);
```

This evaluates to "Length". To return "StringBuilder.Length", you would do this:

```
nameof(StringBuilder)+"."+nameof(StringBuilder.Length);
```

Inheritance

A class can *inherit* from another class to extend or customize the original class. Inheriting from a class lets you reuse the functionality in that class instead of building it from scratch. A class can inherit from only a single class but can itself be inherited by many classes, thus forming a class hierarchy. In this example, we begin by defining a class called Asset:

```
public class Asset { public string Name; }
```

Next, we define classes called Stock and House, which inherit from Asset. Stock and House get everything an Asset has, plus any additional members that they define:

```
public class Stock : Asset    // inherits from Asset
{
  public long SharesOwned;
}

public class House : Asset    // inherits from Asset
{
  public decimal Mortgage;
}
```

Here's how we can use these classes:

```
Stock msft = new Stock { Name="MSFT",
                         SharesOwned=1000 };

Console.WriteLine (msft.Name);        // MSFT
Console.WriteLine (msft.SharesOwned); // 1000

House mansion = new House { Name="Mansion",
                            Mortgage=250000 };

Console.WriteLine (mansion.Name);     // Mansion
Console.WriteLine (mansion.Mortgage); // 250000
```

The *subclasses*, Stock and House, inherit the Name field from the *base class*, Asset.

Subclasses are also called *derived classes*.

Polymorphism

References are *polymorphic*. This means a variable of type x can refer to an object that subclasses x. For instance, consider the following method:

```
public static void Display (Asset asset)
{
  System.Console.WriteLine (asset.Name);
}
```

This method can display both a Stock and a House because they are both Assets. Polymorphism works on the basis that subclasses (Stock and House) have all the features of their base class (Asset). The converse, however, is not true. If Display were rewritten to accept a House, you could not pass in an Asset.

Casting and Reference Conversions

An object reference can be:

- Implicitly *upcast* to a base class reference
- Explicitly *downcast* to a subclass reference

Upcasting and downcasting between compatible reference types performs *reference conversions*: a new reference is created that points to the *same* object. An upcast always succeeds; a downcast succeeds only if the object is suitably typed.

Upcasting

An upcast operation creates a base class reference from a subclass reference. For example:

```
Stock msft = new Stock();   // From previous example
Asset a = msft;             // Upcast
```

After the upcast, variable a still references the same Stock object as variable msft. The object being referenced is not itself altered or converted:

```
Console.WriteLine (a == msft);      // True
```

Although a and msft refer to the same object, a has a more restrictive view on that object:

```
Console.WriteLine (a.Name);         // OK
Console.WriteLine (a.SharesOwned);  // Compile-time error
```

The last line generates a compile-time error because the variable a is of type Asset, even though it refers to an object of type Stock. To get to its SharesOwned field, you must *downcast* the Asset to a Stock.

Downcasting

A downcast operation creates a subclass reference from a base class reference. For example:

```
Stock msft = new Stock();
Asset a = msft;                     // Upcast
Stock s = (Stock)a;                 // Downcast
Console.WriteLine (s.SharesOwned);  // <No error>
Console.WriteLine (s == a);         // True
Console.WriteLine (s == msft);      // True
```

As with an upcast, only references are affected—not the underlying object. A downcast requires an explicit cast because it can potentially fail at runtime:

```
House h = new House();
Asset a = h;          // Upcast always succeeds
Stock s = (Stock)a;   // Downcast fails: a is not a Stock
```

If a downcast fails, an InvalidCastException is thrown. This is an example of *runtime type checking* (see "Static and Runtime Type Checking" on page 108).

The as operator

The as operator performs a downcast that evaluates to null (rather than throwing an exception) if the downcast fails:

```
Asset a = new Asset();
Stock s = a as Stock;   // s is null; no exception thrown
```

This is useful when you're going to subsequently test whether the result is null:

```
if (s != null) Console.WriteLine (s.SharesOwned);
```

The as operator cannot perform *custom conversions* (see "Operator Overloading" on page 226), and it cannot do numeric conversions.

The is operator

The is operator tests whether a reference conversion would succeed—in other words, whether an object derives from a specified class (or implements an interface). It is often used to test before downcasting:

```
if (a is Stock) Console.Write (((Stock)a).SharesOwned);
```

The is operator also evaluates to true if an unboxing conversion would succeed (see "The object Type" on page 106). However, it does not consider custom or numeric conversions.

From C# 7, you can introduce a variable while using the is operator:

```
if (a is Stock s)
  Console.WriteLine (s.SharesOwned);
```

The variable that you introduce is available for "immediate" consumption and remains in scope outside the is expression:

```
if (a is Stock s && s.SharesOwned > 100000)
  Console.WriteLine ("Wealthy");
else
  s = new Stock();   // s is in scope

Console.WriteLine (s.SharesOwned);  // Still in scope
```

The is operator works with other patterns introduced in recent versions of C#. For a full discussion, see "Patterns" on page 187.

Virtual Function Members

A function marked as virtual can be *overridden* by subclasses wanting to provide a specialized implementation. Methods, properties, indexers, and events can all be declared virtual:

```
public class Asset
{
  public string Name;
  public virtual decimal Liability => 0;
}
```

(Liability => 0 is a shortcut for { get { return 0; } }. See "Expression-bodied properties" on page 82 for more details on this syntax.) A subclass overrides a virtual method by applying the override modifier:

```
public class House : Asset
{
  public decimal Mortgage;

  public override decimal Liability => Mortgage;
}
```

By default, the Liability of an Asset is 0. A Stock does not
need to specialize this behavior. However, the House specializes
the Liability property to return the value of the Mortgage:

```
House mansion = new House { Name="Mansion",
                            Mortgage=250000 };
Asset a = mansion;
Console.WriteLine (mansion.Liability);   // 250000
Console.WriteLine (a.Liability);         // 250000
```

The signatures, return types, and accessibility of the virtual and
overridden methods must be identical. An overridden method
can call its base class implementation via the base keyword (see
"The base Keyword" on page 102).

Covariant returns

From C# 9, you can override a method (or property get accessor) such that it returns a *more derived* (subclassed) type. For
example, you can write a Clone method in the Asset class that
returns an Asset and override that method in the House class
such that it returns a House.

This is permitted because it does not break the contract that
Clone must return an Asset: it returns a House, which *is* an
Asset (and more).

Abstract Classes and Abstract Members

A class declared as *abstract* can never be instantiated. Instead,
only its concrete *subclasses* can be instantiated.

Abstract classes are able to define *abstract members*. Abstract
members are like virtual members, except they don't provide a default implementation. That implementation must be

provided by the subclass, unless that subclass is also declared abstract:

```
public abstract class Asset
{
  // Note empty implementation
  public abstract decimal NetValue { get; }
}
```

Subclasses override abstract members just as though they were virtual.

Hiding Inherited Members

A base class and a subclass can define identical members. For example:

```
public class A      { public int Counter = 1; }
public class B : A  { public int Counter = 2; }
```

The Counter field in class B is said to *hide* the Counter field in class A. Usually, this happens by accident, when a member is added to the base type *after* an identical member was added to the subtype. For this reason, the compiler generates a warning and then resolves the ambiguity as follows:

- References to A (at compile time) bind to A.Counter.

- References to B (at compile time) bind to B.Counter.

Occasionally, you want to hide a member deliberately, in which case you can apply the new modifier to the member in the subclass. The new modifier does nothing more than suppress the compiler warning that would otherwise result:

```
public class A      { public     int Counter = 1; }
public class B : A  { public new int Counter = 2; }
```

The new modifier communicates your intent to the compiler—and other programmers—that the duplicate member is not an accident.

Sealing Functions and Classes

An overridden function member can *seal* its implementation with the `sealed` keyword to prevent it from being overridden by further subclasses. In our earlier virtual function member example, we could have sealed House's implementation of Liability, preventing a class that derives from House from overriding Liability, as follows:

```
public sealed override decimal Liability { get { ... } }
```

You can also apply the `sealed` modifier to the class itself, to prevent subclassing.

The base Keyword

The `base` keyword is similar to the `this` keyword. It serves two essential purposes: accessing an overridden function member from the subclass and calling a base class constructor (see the next section).

In this example, House uses the `base` keyword to access Asset's implementation of Liability:

```
public class House : Asset
{
  ...
  public override decimal Liability
    => base.Liability + Mortgage;
}
```

With the `base` keyword, we access Asset's Liability property *nonvirtually*. This means that we will always access Asset's version of this property, regardless of the instance's actual runtime type.

The same approach works if Liability is *hidden* rather than *overridden*. (You can also access hidden members by casting to the base class before invoking the function.)

Constructors and Inheritance

A subclass must declare its own constructors. For example, assume we define `Baseclass` and `Subclass` as follows:

```
public class Baseclass
{
  public int X;
  public Baseclass () { }
  public Baseclass (int x) => X = x;
}
public class Subclass : Baseclass { }
```

The following is then illegal:

```
Subclass s = new Subclass (123);
```

`Subclass` must "redefine" any constructors that it wants to expose. In doing so, it can call any of the base class's constructors with the `base` keyword:

```
public class Subclass : Baseclass
{
  public Subclass (int x) : base (x) { ... }
}
```

The `base` keyword works rather like the `this` keyword, except that it calls a constructor in the base class. Base class constructors always execute first; this ensures that *base* initialization occurs before *specialized* initialization.

If a constructor in a subclass omits the `base` keyword, the base type's *parameterless* constructor is implicitly called (if the base class has no accessible parameterless constructor, the compiler generates an error).

Required members (C# 11)

The requirement for subclasses to invoke a constructor in the base class can become burdensome in large class hierarchies if there are many constructors with many parameters. Sometimes, the best solution is to avoid constructors altogether and rely solely on object initializers to set fields or properties during construction. To help with this, you can mark a field or property as required (from C# 11):

```
public class Asset
{
  public required string Name;
}
```

A required member *must* be populated via an object initializer when constructed:

```
Asset a1 = new Asset { Name="House" };  // OK
Asset a2 = new Asset();                 // Error
```

Should you wish to also write a constructor, you can apply the [SetsRequiredMembers] attribute to bypass the required member restriction for that constructor:

```
public class Asset
{
  public required string Name;

  public Asset() { }

  [System.Diagnostics.CodeAnalysis.SetsRequiredMembers]
  public Asset (string n) => Name = n;
}
```

Constructor and field initialization order

When an object is instantiated, initialization takes place in the following order:

1. From subclass to base class:
   a. Fields are initialized.

   b. Arguments to base class constructor calls are evaluated.

2. From base class to subclass:
   c. Constructor bodies execute.

Inheritance with primary constructors

Classes with primary constructors can subclass with the following syntax:

```
class Baseclass (int x) {...}
class Subclass (int x, int y) : Baseclass (x) {...}
```

Overloading and Resolution

Inheritance has an interesting impact on method overloading. Consider the following two overloads:

```
static void Foo (Asset a) { }
static void Foo (House h) { }
```

When an overload is called, the most specific type has precedence:

```
House h = new House (...);
Foo(h);                        // Calls Foo(House)
```

The particular overload to call is determined statically (at compile time) rather than at runtime. The following code calls Foo(Asset), even though the runtime type of a is House:

```
Asset a = new House (...);
Foo(a);                        // Calls Foo(Asset)
```

NOTE

If you cast Asset to dynamic (see "Dynamic Binding" on page 218), the decision as to which overload to call is deferred until runtime and is based on the object's actual type.

The object Type

object (System.Object) is the ultimate base class for all types. Any type can be implicitly upcast to object.

To illustrate how this is useful, consider a general-purpose *stack*. A stack is a data structure based on the principle of LIFO —"last in, first out." A stack has two operations: *push* an object on the stack and *pop* an object off the stack. Here is a simple implementation that can hold up to 10 objects:

```
public class Stack
{
  int position;
  object[] data = new object[10];
  public void Push (object o) { data[position++] = o; }
  public object Pop() { return data[--position]; }
}
```

Because Stack works with the object type, we can Push and Pop instances of *any type* to and from the Stack:

```
Stack stack = new Stack();
stack.Push ("sausage");
string s = (string) stack.Pop();   // Downcast
Console.WriteLine (s);             // sausage
```

object is a reference type, by virtue of being a class. Despite this, value types, such as int, can also be cast to and from object. To make this possible, the CLR must perform some special work to bridge the underlying differences between value and reference types. This process is called *boxing* and *unboxing*.

NOTE

In "Generics" on page 124, we describe how to improve our Stack class to better handle stacks with same-typed elements.

Boxing and Unboxing

Boxing is the act of casting a value type instance to a reference type instance. The reference type can be either the object class or an interface (see "Interfaces" on page 115). In this example, we box an int into an object:

```
int x = 9;
object obj = x;          // Box the int
```

Unboxing reverses the operation by casting the object back to the original value type:

```
int y = (int)obj;        // Unbox the int
```

Unboxing requires an explicit cast. The runtime checks that the stated value type matches the actual object type, throwing an InvalidCastException if the check fails. For instance, the following throws an exception because long does not exactly match int:

```
object obj = 9;       // 9 is inferred to be of type int
long x = (long) obj;  // InvalidCastException
```

The following succeeds, however:

```
object obj = 9;
long x = (int) obj;
```

As does this:

```
object obj = 3.5;        // 3.5 inferred to be type double
int x = (int) (double) obj;   // x is now 3
```

In the last example, (double) performs an *unboxing*, and then (int) performs a *numeric conversion*.

Boxing *copies* the value type instance into the new object, and unboxing *copies* the contents of the object back into a value type instance:

```
int i = 3;
object boxed = i;
i = 5;
Console.WriteLine (boxed);    // 3
```

Static and Runtime Type Checking

C# checks types both statically (at compile time) and at run-time.

Static type checking enables the compiler to verify the correctness of your program without running it. The following code will fail because the compiler enforces static typing:

```
int x = "5";
```

Runtime type checking is performed by the CLR when you downcast via a reference conversion or unboxing:

```
object y = "5";
int z = (int) y;        // Runtime error, downcast failed
```

Runtime type checking is possible because each object on the heap internally stores a little type token. You can retrieve this token by calling the GetType method of object.

The GetType Method and typeof Operator

All types in C# are represented at runtime with an instance of System.Type. There are two basic ways to get a System.Type object: call GetType on the instance or use the typeof operator on a type name. GetType is evaluated at runtime; typeof is evaluated statically at compile time.

System.Type has properties for such things as the type's name, assembly, base type, and so on. For example:

```
int x = 3;

Console.Write (x.GetType().Name);           // Int32
Console.Write (typeof(int).Name);           // Int32
Console.Write (x.GetType().FullName);    // System.Int32
Console.Write (x.GetType() == typeof(int));    // True
```

System.Type also has methods that act as a gateway to the runtime's reflection model—we describe this fully in *C# 12 in a Nutshell*.

Object Member Listing

Here are all the members of object:

```
public extern Type GetType();
public virtual bool Equals (object obj);
public static bool Equals (object objA, object objB);
public static bool ReferenceEquals (object objA,
                                    object objB);
public virtual int GetHashCode();
public virtual string ToString();
protected virtual void Finalize();
protected extern object MemberwiseClone();
```

Equals, ReferenceEquals, and GetHashCode

The Equals method in the object class is similar to the ==
operator except that Equals is virtual, whereas == is static. The
following example illustrates the difference:

```
object x = 3;
object y = 3;
Console.WriteLine (x == y);       // False
Console.WriteLine (x.Equals (y)); // True
```

Because x and y have been cast to the object type, the compiler
statically binds to object's == operator, which uses *reference
type* semantics to compare two instances. (And because x and
y are boxed, they are represented in separate memory locations
and so are unequal.) The virtual Equals method, however,
defers to the Int32 type's Equals method, which uses *value type*
semantics in comparing two values.

The static object.Equals method simply calls the virtual
Equals method on the first argument—after checking that the
arguments are not null:

```
object x = null, y = 3;
bool error = x.Equals (y);        // Runtime error!
bool ok = object.Equals (x, y);   // OK (false)
```

ReferenceEquals forces a reference type equality comparison
(this is occasionally useful on reference types for which the ==
operator has been overloaded to do otherwise).

`GetHashCode` emits a hash code suitable for use with hashtable-based dictionaries such as `System.Collections.Generic.Dictio nary` and `System.Collections.Hashtable`.

To customize a type's equality semantics, you must at a minimum override `Equals` and `GetHashCode`. You would also usually overload the `==` and `!=` operators. For an example of how to do both, see "Operator Overloading" on page 226.

The ToString Method

The `ToString` method returns the default textual representation of a type instance. The `ToString` method is overridden by all built-in types:

```
string s1 = 1.ToString();      // s1 is "1"
string s2 = true.ToString();   // s2 is "True"
```

You can override the `ToString` method on custom types as follows:

```
public override string ToString() => "Foo";
```

Structs

A *struct* is similar to a class, with the following key differences:

- A struct is a value type, whereas a class is a reference type.
- A struct does not support inheritance (other than implicitly deriving from `object`, or more precisely, `System.Value Type`).

A struct can have all the members that a class can, except for a finalizer, and virtual or protected members.

A struct is appropriate when value type semantics are desirable. Good examples are numeric types, where it is more natural for assignment to copy a value rather than a reference. Because a struct is a value type, each instance does not require instantiation of an object on the heap (and subsequent collection); this can incur useful savings when you're creating many instances of a type.

As with any value type, a struct can end up on the heap indirectly, either through boxing or by appearing as a field in a class. If we were to instantiate SomeClass in the following example, field Y would refer to a struct on the heap:

```
struct SomeStruct { public int X;        }
class SomeClass  { public SomeStruct Y; }
```

Similarly, if you were to declare an array of SomeStruct, the instance would reside on the heap (because arrays are reference types), although the entire array would require only a single memory allocation.

From C# 7.2, you can apply the ref modifier to a struct to ensure that it can be used only in ways that will place it on the stack. This enables further compiler optimizations as well as allowing for the Span<T> type (*https://oreil.ly/kCark*).

Struct Construction Semantics

NOTE

Prior to C# 11, every field in a struct had to be explicitly assigned in the constructor (or field initializer). This restriction has now been relaxed.

In addition to any constructors that you define, a struct always has an implicit parameterless constructor that performs a bitwise-zeroing of its fields (setting them to their default values):

```
Point p = new Point();     // p.x and p.y will be 0
struct Point { int x, y; }
```

Even when you define a parameterless constructor of your own, the implicit parameterless constructor still exists, and it can be accessed via the default keyword:

```
Point p1 = new Point();     // p1.x and p1.y will be 1
Point p2 = default;         // p2.x and p2.y will be 0

struct Point
{
  int x = 1; int y;
  public Point() => y = 1;
}
```

In this example, we initialized x to 1 via a field initializer, and we initialized y to 1 via the parameterless constructor. And yet with the default keyword, we were still able to create a Point that bypassed both initializations. The default constructor can be accessed other ways, too, as the following example illustrates:

```
var points = new Point[10];   // Each point will be (0,0)
var test = new Test();        // test.p will be (0,0)
class Test { Point p; }
```

A good strategy with structs is to design them such that their `default` value is a valid state, thereby making initialization redundant.

readonly Structs and Functions

You can apply the `readonly` modifier to a struct to enforce that all fields are `readonly`; this aids in declaring intent as well as allowing the compiler more optimization freedom:

```
readonly struct Point
{
  public readonly int X, Y;   // X and Y must be readonly
}
```

If you need to apply `readonly` at a more granular level, you can apply the `readonly` modifier (from C# 8) to a struct's *functions*. This ensures that if the function attempts to modify any field, a compile-time error is generated:

```
struct Point
{
  public int X, Y;
  public readonly void ResetX() => X = 0;  // Error!
}
```

If a `readonly` function calls a non-`readonly` function, the compiler generates a warning (and defensively copies the struct to avoid the possibility of a mutation).

Access Modifiers

To promote encapsulation, a type or type member can limit its *accessibility* to other types and other assemblies by adding an *access modifier* to the declaration:

public
> Fully accessible. This is the implicit accessibility for members of an enum or interface.

`internal`

> Accessible only within the containing assembly or friend assemblies. This is the default accessibility for non-nested types.

`private`

> Accessible only within the containing type. This is the default accessibility for members of a class or struct.

`protected`

> Accessible only within the containing type or subclasses.

`protected internal`

> The *union* of `protected` and `internal` accessibility (this is more *permissive* than `protected` or `internal` alone in that it makes a member more accessible in two ways).

`private protected`

> The *intersection* of `protected` and `internal` accessibility (this is more *restrictive* than `protected` or `internal` alone).

`file` *(from C# 11)*

> Accessible only from within the same file. Intended for use by *source generators* (see "Extended partial methods" on page 94). This modifier can be applied only to type declarations.

In the following example, `Class2` is accessible from outside its assembly; `Class1` is not:

```
class Class1 {}          // Class1 is internal (default)
public class Class2 {}
```

`ClassB` exposes field x to other types in the same assembly; `ClassA` does not:

```
class ClassA { int x;          } // x is private
class ClassB { internal int x; }
```

When you're overriding a base class function, accessibility must be identical on the overridden function. The compiler prevents any inconsistent use of access modifiers—for example, a subclass itself can be less accessible than a base class but not more.

Friend Assemblies

You can expose `internal` members to other *friend* assemblies by adding the `System.Runtime.CompilerServices.InternalsVi sibleTo` assembly attribute, specifying the name of the friend assembly as follows:

```
[assembly: InternalsVisibleTo ("Friend")]
```

If the friend assembly is signed with a strong name, you must specify its *full* 160-byte public key. You can extract this key via a Language Integrated Query (LINQ)—an interactive example is given in LINQPad's free sample library for *C# 12 in a Nutshell*, under Chapter 3, "Access Modifiers."

Accessibility Capping

A type caps the accessibility of its declared members. The most common example of capping is when you have an `internal` type with `public` members. For example:

```
class C { public void Foo() {} }
```

C's (default) `internal` accessibility caps Foo's accessibility, effectively making `Foo` `internal`. A common reason `Foo` would be marked `public` is to make for easier refactoring, should `C` later be changed to `public`.

Interfaces

An *interface* is similar to a class but only *specifies behavior* and does not hold state (data). Consequently:

- Interface members are *all implicitly abstract*. (There are exceptions to this rule that we will describe in "Default Interface Members" on page 119 and "Static Interface Members" on page 120.)

- A class (or struct) can implement *multiple* interfaces. In contrast, a class can inherit from only a *single* class, and a struct cannot inherit at all (aside from deriving from System.ValueType).

An interface declaration is like a class declaration, but it (normally) provides no implementation for its members, because all its members are implicitly abstract. These members will be implemented by the classes and structs that implement the interface. An interface can contain only methods, properties, events, and indexers, which not coincidentally are precisely the members of a class that can be abstract.

Here is a slightly simplified version of the IEnumerator interface, defined in System.Collections:

```
public interface IEnumerator
{
  bool MoveNext();
  object Current { get; }
  void Reset();
}
```

Interface members are always implicitly public and cannot declare an access modifier. Implementing an interface means providing a public implementation for all of its members:

```
internal class Countdown : IEnumerator
{
  int count = 6;
  public bool MoveNext()  => count-- > 0 ;
  public object Current   => count;
  public void Reset()     => count = 6;
}
```

You can implicitly cast an object to any interface that it implements:

```
IEnumerator e = new Countdown();
while (e.MoveNext())
  Console.Write (e.Current + " ");  // 5 4 3 2 1 0
```

Extending an Interface

Interfaces can derive from other interfaces. For instance:

```
public interface IUndoable            { void Undo(); }
public interface IRedoable : IUndoable { void Redo(); }
```

IRedoable "inherits" all the members of IUndoable.

Explicit Interface Implementation

Implementing multiple interfaces can sometimes result in a collision between member signatures. You can resolve such collisions by *explicitly implementing* an interface member. For example:

```
interface I1 { void Foo(); }
interface I2 { int Foo();  }

public class Widget : I1, I2
{
  public void Foo()   // Implicit implementation
  {
    Console.Write ("Widget's implementation of I1.Foo");
  }

  int I2.Foo()   // Explicit implementation of I2.Foo
  {
    Console.Write ("Widget's implementation of I2.Foo");
    return 42;
  }
}
```

Because both I1 and I2 have conflicting Foo signatures, Widget explicitly implements I2's Foo method. This lets the two methods coexist in one class. The only way to call an explicitly implemented member is to cast to its interface:

```
Widget w = new Widget();
w.Foo();            // Widget's implementation of I1.Foo
((I1)w).Foo();      // Widget's implementation of I1.Foo
((I2)w).Foo();      // Widget's implementation of I2.Foo
```

Another reason to explicitly implement interface members is to hide members that are highly specialized and distracting to a type's normal use case. For example, a type that implements ISerializable would typically want to avoid flaunting its ISerializable members unless explicitly cast to that interface.

Implementing Interface Members Virtually

An implicitly implemented interface member is, by default, sealed. It must be marked virtual or abstract in the base class in order to be overridden: calling the interface member through either the base class or the interface then calls the subclass's implementation.

An explicitly implemented interface member cannot be marked virtual, nor can it be overridden in the usual manner. It can, however, be *reimplemented*.

Reimplementing an Interface in a Subclass

A subclass can *reimplement* any interface member already implemented by a base class. Reimplementation hijacks a member implementation (when called through the interface) and works whether or not the member is virtual in the base class.

In the following example, TextBox implements IUndoable.Undo explicitly, and so it cannot be marked as virtual. To "override" it, RichTextBox must reimplement IUndoable's Undo method:

```
public interface IUndoable { void Undo(); }

public class TextBox : IUndoable
{
  void IUndoable.Undo()
    => Console.WriteLine ("TextBox.Undo");
}

public class RichTextBox : TextBox, IUndoable
{
  public new void Undo()
    => Console.WriteLine ("RichTextBox.Undo");
}
```

Calling the reimplemented member through the interface calls the subclass's implementation:

```
RichTextBox r = new RichTextBox();
r.Undo();                   // RichTextBox.Undo
((IUndoable)r).Undo();    // RichTextBox.Undo
```

In this case, TextBox implements the Undo method explicitly. If TextBox instead implemented the Undo method implicitly, RichTextBox could still reimplement the method, but the effects would be nonpervasive in that calling the member through the base class would invoke the base implementation:

```
RichTextBox r = new RichTextBox();
((TextBox)r).Undo();        // TextBox.Undo
```

Default Interface Members

From C# 8, you can add a default implementation to an interface member, making it optional to implement:

```
interface ILogger
{
  void Log (string text) => Console.WriteLine (text);
}
```

This is advantageous if you wish to add a member to an interface defined in a popular library without breaking (potentially thousands of) implementations.

Default implementations are always explicit, so if a class implementing ILogger fails to define a Log method, the only way to call it is through the interface:

```
class Logger : ILogger { }
...
((ILogger)new Logger()).Log ("message");
```

This prevents a problem of multiple implementation inheritance: if the same default member is added to two interfaces that a class implements, there is never an ambiguity as to which member is called.

Static Interface Members

An interface can also declare static members. There are two kinds of static interface members:

- Static nonvirtual interface members
- Static virtual/abstract interface members

Static nonvirtual interface members

Static nonvirtual interface members exist mainly to help with writing default interface members. They are not implemented by classes or structs; instead, they are consumed directly. Along with methods, properties, events, and indexers, static nonvirtual members permit fields, which are typically accessed from code inside default member implementations:

```
interface ILogger
{
  void Log (string text) =>
    Console.WriteLine (Prefix + text);

  static string Prefix = "";
}
```

Static nonvirtual interface members are public by default, so they can be accessed from the outside:

```
ILogger.Prefix = "File log: ";
```

You can restrict this by adding an accessibility modifier (such as `private`, `protected`, or `internal`).

Instance fields are (still) prohibited. This is in line with the principle of interfaces, which is to define *behavior*, not *state*.

Static virtual/abstract interface members

Static virtual/abstract interface members (from C# 11) are marked with `static abstract` or `static virtual` and enable *static polymorphism*, an advanced feature that we will discuss fully in "Static Polymorphism" on page 247:

```
interface ITypeDescribable
{
  static abstract string Description { get; }
  static virtual string Category => null;
}
```

An implementing class or struct must implement static abstract members and can optionally implement static virtual members:

```
class CustomerTest : ITypeDescribable
{
  public static string Description => "Customer tests";
  public static string Category    => "Unit testing";
}
```

In addition to methods, properties, and events, operators and conversions are also legal targets for static virtual interface members (see "Operator Overloading" on page 226). Static virtual interface members are called through a constrained type parameter; we will demonstrate this in "Static Polymorphism" on page 247 and "Generic Math" on page 249, after covering generics.

Enums

An *enum* is a special value type that lets you specify a group of named numeric constants. For example:

```
public enum BorderSide { Left, Right, Top, Bottom }
```

We can use this enum type as follows:

```
BorderSide topSide = BorderSide.Top;
bool isTop = (topSide == BorderSide.Top);   // true
```

Each enum member has an underlying integral-type value. By default, the underlying values are of type int, and the enum members are assigned the constants 0, 1, 2... (in their declaration order). You may specify an alternative integral type, as follows:

```
public enum BorderSide : byte { Left,Right,Top,Bottom }
```

You may also specify an explicit integer value for each member:

```
public enum BorderSide : byte
  { Left=1, Right=2, Top=10, Bottom=11 }
```

The compiler also lets you explicitly assign *some* of the enum members. The unassigned enum members keep incrementing from the last explicit value. The preceding example is equivalent to:

```
public enum BorderSide : byte
  { Left=1, Right, Top=10, Bottom }
```

Enum Conversions

You can convert an `enum` instance to and from its underlying integral value with an explicit cast:

```
int i = (int) BorderSide.Left;
BorderSide side = (BorderSide) i;
bool leftOrRight = (int) side <= 2;
```

You can also explicitly cast one enum type to another; the translation then uses the members' underlying integral values.

The numeric literal 0 is treated specially in that it does not require an explicit cast:

```
BorderSide b = 0;     // No cast required
if (b == 0) ...
```

In this particular example, `BorderSide` has no member with an integer value of 0. This does not generate an error: a limitation of enums is that the compiler and CLR do not prevent the assignment of integrals whose values fall outside the range of members:

```
BorderSide b = (BorderSide) 12345;
Console.WriteLine (b);            // 12345
```

Flags Enums

You can combine enum members. To prevent ambiguities, members of a combinable enum require explicitly assigned values, typically in powers of two. For example:

```
[Flags]
public enum BorderSides
 { None=0, Left=1, Right=2, Top=4, Bottom=8 }
```

By convention, a combinable enum type is given a plural rather
than singular name. To work with combined enum values, you
use bitwise operators, such as | and &. These operate on the
underlying integral values:

```
BorderSides leftRight =
  BorderSides.Left | BorderSides.Right;

if ((leftRight & BorderSides.Left) != 0)
  Console.WriteLine ("Includes Left");   // Includes Left

string formatted = leftRight.ToString(); // "Left, Right"

BorderSides s = BorderSides.Left;
s |= BorderSides.Right;
Console.WriteLine (s == leftRight);       // True
```

The Flags attribute should be applied to combinable enum
types; if you fail to do this, calling ToString on an enum instance
emits a number rather than a series of names.

For convenience, you can include combination members
within an enum declaration itself:

```
[Flags] public enum BorderSides
{
  None=0,
  Left=1, Right=2, Top=4, Bottom=8,
  LeftRight = Left | Right,
  TopBottom = Top  | Bottom,
  All       = LeftRight | TopBottom
}
```

Enum Operators

The operators that work with enums are:

```
=   ==   !=   <   >   <=   >=   +   -   ^   &   |   ~
+=  -=   ++   --   sizeof
```

The bitwise, arithmetic, and comparison operators return the
result of processing the underlying integral values. Addition

is permitted between an enum and an integral type, but not between two enums.

Nested Types

A *nested type* is declared within the scope of another type. For example:

```
public class TopLevel
{
  public class Nested { }               // Nested class
  public enum Color { Red, Blue, Tan }  // Nested enum
}
```

A nested type has the following features:

- It can access the enclosing type's private members and everything else the enclosing type can access.

- It can be declared with the full range of access modifiers, rather than just public and internal.

- The default accessibility for a nested type is private rather than internal.

- Accessing a nested type from outside the enclosing type requires qualification with the enclosing type's name (like when you're accessing static members).

For example, to access Color.Red from outside our TopLevel class, you'd need to do this:

```
TopLevel.Color color = TopLevel.Color.Red;
```

All types can be nested; however, only classes and structs can nest.

Generics

C# has two separate mechanisms for writing code that are reusable across different types: *inheritance* and *generics*. Whereas inheritance expresses reusability with a base type, generics express reusability with a "template" that contains "placeholder" types. Generics, when compared to inheritance, can *increase type safety* and *reduce casting and boxing*.

Generic Types

A *generic type* declares *type parameters*—placeholder types to be filled in by the consumer of the generic type, which supplies the *type arguments*. Here is a generic type, Stack<T>, designed to stack instances of type T. Stack<T> declares a single type parameter T:

```
public class Stack<T>
{
  int position;
  T[] data = new T[100];
  public void Push (T obj) => data[position++] = obj;
  public T Pop()          => data[--position];
}
```

We can use Stack<T> as follows:

```
var stack = new Stack<int>();
stack.Push (5);
stack.Push (10);
int x = stack.Pop();        // x is 10
int y = stack.Pop();        // y is 5
```

NOTE

Notice that no downcasts are required in the last two lines, avoiding the possibility of a runtime error and eliminating the overhead of boxing/unboxing. This makes our generic stack superior to a nongeneric stack that uses object in place of T (see "The object Type" on page 106 for an example).

Stack<int> fills in the type parameter T with the type argument int, implicitly creating a type on the fly (the synthesis occurs at runtime). Stack<int> effectively has the following definition (substitutions appear in bold, with the class name hashed out to avoid confusion):

```
public class ###
{
  int position;
  int[] data = new int[100];
  public void Push (int obj) => data[position++] = obj;
  public int Pop()          => data[--position];
}
```

Technically, we say that Stack<T> is an *open type*, whereas Stack<int> is a *closed type*. At runtime, all generic type instances are closed—with the placeholder types filled in.

Generic Methods

A *generic method* declares type parameters within the signature of a method. With generic methods, many fundamental algorithms can be implemented in a general-purpose way. Here is a generic method that swaps the contents of two variables of any type T:

```
static void Swap<T> (ref T a, ref T b)
{
  T temp = a; a = b; b = temp;
}
```

You can use Swap<T> as follows:

```
int x = 5, y = 10;
Swap (ref x, ref y);
```

Generally, there is no need to supply type arguments to a generic method, because the compiler can implicitly infer the type. If there is ambiguity, generic methods can be called with the type arguments as follows:

```
Swap<int> (ref x, ref y);
```

Within a generic *type*, a method is not classed as generic unless it *introduces* type parameters (with the angle bracket syntax). The Pop method in our generic stack merely consumes the type's existing type parameter, T, and is not classed as a generic method.

Methods and types are the only constructs that can introduce type parameters. Properties, indexers, events, fields, constructors, operators, and so on cannot declare type parameters, although they can partake in any type parameters already declared by their enclosing type. In our generic stack example, for instance, we could write an indexer that returns a generic item:

```
public T this [int index] { get { return data[index]; } }
```

Similarly, constructors can partake in existing type parameters but cannot *introduce* them.

Declaring Type Parameters

Type parameters can be introduced in the declaration of classes, structs, interfaces, delegates (see "Delegates" on page 134), and methods. You can specify multiple type parameters by separating them with commas:

```
class Dictionary<TKey, TValue> {...}
```

To instantiate:

```
var myDict = new Dictionary<int,string>();
```

Generic type names and method names can be overloaded as long as the number of type parameters differs. For example, the following three type names do not conflict:

```
class A {}
class A<T> {}
class A<T1,T2> {}
```

NOTE

By convention, generic types and methods with a *single* type parameter name their parameter T, as long as the intent of the parameter is clear. With *multiple* type parameters, each parameter has a more descriptive name (prefixed by T).

typeof and Unbound Generic Types

Open generic types do not exist at runtime: open generic types are closed as part of compilation. However, it is possible for an *unbound* generic type to exist at runtime—purely as a Type object. The only way to specify an unbound generic type in C# is with the typeof operator:

```
class A<T> {}
class A<T1,T2> {}
...

Type a1 = typeof (A<>);    // Unbound type
Type a2 = typeof (A<,>);   // Indicates 2 type args
Console.Write (a2.GetGenericArguments().Count()); // 2
```

You can also use the typeof operator to specify a closed type:

```
Type a3 = typeof (A<int,int>);
```

It can specify an open type as well (which is closed at runtime):

```
class B<T> { void X() { Type t = typeof (T); } }
```

The default Generic Value

You can use the default keyword to get the default value for a generic type parameter. The default value for a reference type is null, and the default value for a value type is the result of bitwise-zeroing the type's fields:

```
static void Zap<T> (T[] array)
{
  for (int i = 0; i < array.Length; i++)
    array[i] = default(T);
}
```

From C# 7.1, you can omit the type argument for cases in which the compiler is able to infer it:

```
    array[i] = default;
```

Generic Constraints

By default, a type parameter can be substituted with any type whatsoever. *Constraints* can be applied to a type parameter to require more specific type arguments. There are eight kinds of constraints:

```
where T : base-class   // Base class constraint
where T : interface    // Interface constraint
where T : class        // Reference type constraint
where T : class?       // (See "Nullable Reference Types")
where T : struct       // Value type constraint
where T : unmanaged    // Unmanaged constraint
where T : new()        // Parameterless constructor
                       // constraint
where U : T            // Naked type constraint
where T : notnull      // Non-nullable value type
                       // or non-nullable reference type
```

In the following example, GenericClass<T,U> requires T to derive from (or be identical to) SomeClass and implement Interface1, and requires U to provide a parameterless constructor:

```
class       SomeClass {}
interface Interface1 {}

class GenericClass<T,U> where T : SomeClass, Interface1
                        where U : new()
{ ... }
```

Constraints can be applied wherever type parameters are defined, whether in methods or in type definitions.

A *base class constraint* specifies that the type parameter must subclass (or match) a particular class; an *interface constraint* specifies that the type parameter must implement that interface. These constraints allow instances of the type parameter to be implicitly converted to that class or interface.

The *class constraint* and *struct constraint* specify that T must be a reference type or a (non-nullable) value type, respectively. The unmanaged constraint is a stronger version of a struct constraint: T must be a simple value type or a struct that is (recursively) free of any reference types. The *parameterless constructor constraint* requires T to have a public parameterless constructor and allows you to call new() on T:

```
static void Initialize<T> (T[] array) where T : new()
{
  for (int i = 0; i < array.Length; i++)
    array[i] = new T();
}
```

The *naked type constraint* requires one type parameter to derive from (or match) another type parameter.

Subclassing Generic Types

A generic class can be subclassed just like a nongeneric class. The subclass can leave the base class's type parameters open, as in the following example:

```
class Stack<T>                    {...}
class SpecialStack<T> : Stack<T> {...}
```

Or the subclass can close the generic type parameters with a concrete type:

```
class IntStack : Stack<int>  {...}
```

A subtype can also introduce fresh type arguments:

```
class List<T>                     {...}
class KeyedList<T,TKey> : List<T> {...}
```

Self-Referencing Generic Declarations

A type can name *itself* as the concrete type when closing a type argument:

```
public interface IEquatable<T> { bool Equals (T obj); }

public class Balloon : IEquatable<Balloon>
{
  public bool Equals (Balloon b) { ... }
}
```

The following are also legal:

```
class Foo<T> where T : IComparable<T> { ... }
class Bar<T> where T : Bar<T> { ... }
```

Static Data

Static data is unique for each closed type:

```
Console.WriteLine (++Bob<int>.Count);     // 1
Console.WriteLine (++Bob<int>.Count);     // 2
Console.WriteLine (++Bob<string>.Count);  // 1
Console.WriteLine (++Bob<object>.Count);  // 1

class Bob<T> { public static int Count; }
```

Covariance

Assuming A is convertible to B, X has a covariant type parameter
if X<A> is convertible to X<B>.

(With C#'s notion of variance, *convertible* means convertible via
an *implicit reference conversion*—such as A *subclassing* B, or A
implementing B. Numeric conversions, boxing conversions, and
custom conversions are not included.)

For instance, type IFoo<T> has a covariant T if the following is
legal:

```
IFoo<string> s = ...;
IFoo<object> b = s;
```

Interfaces (and delegates) permit covariant type parameters. To
illustrate, suppose that the Stack<T> class that we wrote at the
beginning of this section implements the following interface:

```
public interface IPoppable<out T> { T Pop(); }
```

The out modifier on T indicates that T is used only in *output
positions* (e.g., return types for methods) and flags the type
parameter as *covariant*, permitting the following code:

```
// Assuming that Bear subclasses Animal:
var bears = new Stack<Bear>();
bears.Push (new Bear());

// Because bears implements IPoppable<Bear>,
// we can convert it to IPoppable<Animal>:
```

```
IPoppable<Animal> animals = bears;    // Legal
Animal a = animals.Pop();
```

The cast from bears to animals is permitted by the compiler—
by virtue of the interface's type parameter being covariant.

NOTE

The IEnumerator<T> and IEnumerable<T> interfaces (see
"Enumeration and Iterators" on page 161) are marked
with a covariant T. This allows you to cast IEnumera
ble<string> to IEnumerable<object>, for instance.

The compiler will generate an error if you use a covariant type
parameter in an *input* position (e.g., a parameter to a method
or a writable property). The purpose of this limitation is to
guarantee compile-time type safety. For instance, it prevents
us from adding a Push(T) method to that interface, which
consumers could abuse with the seemingly benign operation
of pushing a camel onto an IPoppable<Animal> (remember that
the underlying type in our example is a stack of bears). To
define a Push(T) method, T must in fact be *contravariant*.

NOTE

C# supports covariance (and contravariance) only for elements with *reference conversions*—not *boxing conversions*.
So, if you wrote a method that accepted a parameter of
type IPoppable<object>, you could call it with IPoppa
ble<string> but not IPoppable<int>.

Contravariance

We previously saw that, assuming that A allows an implicit reference conversion to B, a type X has a covariant type parameter

if X<A> allows a reference conversion to X<B>. A type is *contravariant* when you can convert in the reverse direction—from X<B> to X<A>. This is supported on interfaces and delegates when the type parameter appears only in *input* positions, designated with the `in` modifier. Extending our previous example, if the Stack<T> class implements the following interface:

```
public interface IPushable<in T> { void Push (T obj); }
```

we can legally do this:

```
IPushable<Animal> animals = new Stack<Animal>();
IPushable<Bear> bears = animals;      // Legal
bears.Push (new Bear());
```

Mirroring covariance, the compiler will report an error if you try to use a contravariant type parameter in an output position (e.g., as a return value or in a readable property).

Delegates

A *delegate* wires up a method caller to its target method at runtime. There are two aspects to a delegate: *type* and *instance*. A *delegate type* defines a *protocol* to which the caller and target will conform, comprising a list of parameter types and a return type. A *delegate instance* is an object that refers to one (or more) target methods conforming to that protocol.

A delegate instance literally acts as a delegate for the caller: the caller invokes the delegate, and then the delegate calls the target method. This indirection decouples the caller from the target method.

A delegate type declaration is preceded by the keyword `delegate`, but otherwise it resembles an (abstract) method declaration. For example:

```
delegate int Transformer (int x);
```

To create a delegate instance, you can assign a method to a delegate variable:

```
Transformer t = Square;   // Create delegate instance
int result = t(3);        // Invoke delegate
Console.Write (result);   // 9

int Square (int x) => x * x;
```

Invoking a delegate is just like invoking a method (because the delegate's purpose is merely to provide a level of indirection):

```
t(3);
```

The statement Transformer t = Square is shorthand for the following:

```
Transformer t = new Transformer (Square);
```

And t(3) is shorthand for this:

```
t.Invoke (3);
```

A delegate is similar to a *callback*, a general term that captures constructs such as C function pointers.

Writing Plug-In Methods with Delegates

A delegate variable is assigned a method at runtime. This is useful for writing plug-in methods. In this example, we have a utility method named Transform that applies a transform to each element in an integer array. The Transform method has a delegate parameter for specifying a plug-in transform:

```
int[] values = { 1, 2, 3 };
Transform (values, Square);  // Hook in the Square method

foreach (int i in values)
  Console.Write (i + " ");   // 1   4   9

void Transform (int[] values, Transformer t)
{
  for (int i = 0; i < values.Length; i++)
    values[i] = t (values[i]);
}

int Square (int x) => x * x;

delegate int Transformer (int x);
```

Instance and Static Method Targets

A delegate's target method can be a local, static, or instance method.

When an *instance* method is assigned to a delegate object, the latter must maintain a reference not only to the method but also to the *instance* to which the method belongs. The System.Delegate class's Target property represents this instance (and will be null for a delegate referencing a static method).

Multicast Delegates

All delegate instances have *multicast* capability. This means that a delegate instance can reference not just a single target method but also a list of target methods. The + and += operators combine delegate instances. For example:

```
SomeDelegate d = SomeMethod1;
d += SomeMethod2;
```

The last line is functionally the same as this one:

```
d = d + SomeMethod2;
```

Invoking d will now call both SomeMethod1 and SomeMethod2. Delegates are invoked in the order in which they are added.

The - and -= operators remove the right delegate operand from the left delegate operand. For example:

```
d -= SomeMethod1;
```

Invoking d will now cause only SomeMethod2 to be invoked.

Calling + or += on a delegate variable with a null value is legal, as is calling -= on a delegate variable with a single target (which will result in the delegate instance being null).

If a multicast delegate has a nonvoid return type, the caller receives the return value from the last method to be invoked. The preceding methods are still called, but their return values are discarded. In most scenarios in which multicast delegates are used, they have void return types, so this subtlety does not arise.

All delegate types implicitly derive from System.MulticastDele gate, which inherits from System.Delegate. C# compiles +, -, +=, and -= operations made on a delegate to the static Combine and Remove methods of the System.Delegate class.

Generic Delegate Types

A delegate type can contain generic type parameters. For example:

```
public delegate T Transformer<T> (T arg);
```

Here's how we could use this delegate type:

```
Transformer<double> s = Square;
Console.WriteLine (s (3.3));        // 10.89

double Square (double x) => x * x;
```

The Func and Action Delegates

With generic delegates, it becomes possible to write a small set of delegate types that are so general they can work for methods of any return type and any (reasonable) number of arguments. These delegates are the Func and Action delegates, defined in the System namespace (the in and out annotations indicate *variance*, which we cover in the context of delegates shortly):

```
delegate TResult Func <out TResult> ();
delegate TResult Func <in T, out TResult> (T arg);
delegate TResult Func <in T1, in T2, out TResult>
 (T1 arg1, T2 arg2);
... and so on, up to T16

delegate void Action ();
delegate void Action <in T> (T arg);
delegate void Action <in T1, in T2> (T1 arg1, T2 arg2);
... and so on, up to T16
```

These delegates are extremely general. The `Transformer` delegate in our previous example can be replaced with a `Func` delegate that takes a single argument of type `T` and returns a same-typed value:

```
public static void Transform<T> (
  T[] values, Func<T,T> transformer)
{
  for (int i = 0; i < values.Length; i++)
    values[i] = transformer (values[i]);
}
```

The only practical scenarios not covered by these delegates are `ref`/`out` and pointer parameters.

Delegate Compatibility

Delegate types are all incompatible with one another, even if their signatures are the same:

```
delegate void D1(); delegate void D2();
...
D1 d1 = Method1;
D2 d2 = d1;                // Compile-time error
```

The following, however, is permitted:

```
D2 d2 = new D2 (d1);
```

Delegate instances are considered equal if they have the same type and method target(s). For multicast delegates, the order of the method targets is significant.

Return type variance

When you call a method, you might get back a type that is more specific than what you asked for. This is ordinary polymorphic behavior. In keeping with this, a delegate target method might return a more specific type than described by the delegate. This is *covariance*:

```
ObjectRetriever o = new ObjectRetriever (RetrieveString);
object result = o();
Console.WriteLine (result);       // hello

string RetrieveString() => "hello";

delegate object ObjectRetriever();
```

The ObjectRetriever expects to get back an object, but an object *subclass* will also do because delegate return types are *covariant*.

Parameter variance

When you call a method, you can supply arguments that have more specific types than the parameters of that method. This is ordinary polymorphic behavior. In keeping with this, a delegate target method may have *less* specific parameter types than described by the delegate. This is called *contravariance*:

```
StringAction sa = new StringAction (ActOnObject);
sa ("hello");

void ActOnObject (object o) => Console.WriteLine (o);

delegate void StringAction (string s);
```

NOTE

The standard event pattern is designed to help you take advantage of delegate parameter contravariance through its use of the common EventArgs base class. For example, you can have a single method invoked by two different delegates, one passing a MouseEventArgs and the other passing a KeyEventArgs.

Type parameter variance for generic delegates

We saw in "Generics" on page 124 how type parameters can be covariant and contravariant for generic interfaces. The same capability also exists for generic delegates. If you're defining a generic delegate type, it's a good practice to do the following:

- Mark a type parameter used only on the return value as covariant (out)

- Mark any type parameters used only on parameters as contravariant (in)

Doing so allows conversions to work naturally by respecting inheritance relationships between types. The following delegate (defined in the System namespace) is covariant for TResult:

```
delegate TResult Func<out TResult>();
```

This allows:

```
Func<string> x = ...;
Func<object> y = x;
```

The following delegate (defined in the System namespace) is contravariant for T:

```
delegate void Action<in T> (T arg);
```

This allows:

```
Action<object> x = ...;
Action<string> y = x;
```

Events

When you're using delegates, two emergent roles commonly appear: *broadcaster* and *subscriber*. The *broadcaster* is a type that contains a delegate field. The broadcaster decides when to broadcast, by invoking the delegate. The *subscribers* are the method target recipients. A subscriber decides when to start and stop listening, by calling += and -= on the broadcaster's delegate. A subscriber does not know about, or interfere with, other subscribers.

Events are a language feature that formalizes this pattern. An event is a construct that exposes just the subset of delegate features required for the broadcaster/subscriber model. The main purpose of events is to *prevent subscribers from interfering with one another.*

The easiest way to declare an event is to put the event keyword in front of a delegate member:

```
public class Broadcaster
{
  public event ProgressReporter Progress;
}
```

Code within the Broadcaster type has full access to Progress and can treat it as a delegate. Code outside of Broadcaster can perform only += and -= operations on the Progress event.

In the following example, the Stock class fires its PriceChanged event every time the Price of the Stock changes:

```
public delegate void PriceChangedHandler
 (decimal oldPrice, decimal newPrice);

public class Stock
{
  string symbol; decimal price;

  public Stock (string symbol) => this.symbol = symbol;

  public event PriceChangedHandler PriceChanged;
```

```
public decimal Price
{
  get => price;
  set
  {
    if (price == value) return;
    // Fire event if invocation list isn't empty:
    if (PriceChanged != null)
      PriceChanged (price, value);
    price = value;
  }
}
}
```

If we remove the event keyword from our example so that
PriceChanged becomes an ordinary delegate field, our example
would give the same results. However, Stock would be less
robust in that subscribers could do the following things to
interfere with one another:

- Replace other subscribers by reassigning PriceChanged
  (instead of using the += operator)

- Clear all subscribers (by setting PriceChanged to null)

- Broadcast to other subscribers by invoking the delegate

Events can be virtual, overridden, abstract, or sealed. They can
also be static.

Standard Event Pattern

In almost all cases in which events are defined in the .NET
library, their definition adheres to a standard pattern designed
to provide consistency across library and user code. Here's the
preceding example refactored with this pattern:

```
public class PriceChangedEventArgs : EventArgs
{
  public readonly decimal LastPrice, NewPrice;

  public PriceChangedEventArgs (decimal lastPrice,
                                decimal newPrice)
  {
```

```
    LastPrice = lastPrice; NewPrice = newPrice;
  }
}

public class Stock
{
  string symbol; decimal price;

  public Stock (string symbol) => this.symbol = symbol;

  public event EventHandler<PriceChangedEventArgs>
             PriceChanged;

  protected virtual void OnPriceChanged
                        (PriceChangedEventArgs e) =>
    // Shortcut for invoking PriceChanged if not null:
    PriceChanged?.Invoke (this, e);

  public decimal Price
  {
    get { return price; }
    set
    {
      if (price == value) return;
      OnPriceChanged (new PriceChangedEventArgs (price,
                                                 value));
      price = value;
    }
  }
}
```

At the core of the standard event pattern is System.EventArgs, a predefined .NET class with no members (other than the static Empty field). EventArgs is a base class for conveying information for an event. In this example, we subclass EventArgs to convey the old and new prices when a PriceChanged event is fired.

The generic System.EventHandler delegate is also part of .NET and is defined as follows:

```
public delegate void EventHandler<TEventArgs>
  (object source, TEventArgs e)
```

A protected virtual method named On-*event-name* centralizes firing of the event. This allows subclasses to fire the event (which is usually desirable) and also allows subclasses to insert code before and after the event is fired.

Here's how we could use our Stock class:

```
Stock stock = new Stock ("THPW");
stock.Price = 27.10M;

stock.PriceChanged += stock_PriceChanged;
stock.Price = 31.59M;

static void stock_PriceChanged
  (object sender, PriceChangedEventArgs e)
{
  if ((e.NewPrice - e.LastPrice) / e.LastPrice > 0.1M)
    Console.WriteLine ("Alert, 10% price increase!");
}
```

For events that don't carry additional information, .NET also provides a nongeneric EventHandler delegate. We can demonstrate this by rewriting our Stock class such that the Price Changed event fires *after* the price changes. This means that no additional information need be transmitted with the event:

```
public class Stock
{
  string symbol; decimal price;

  public Stock (string symbol) => this.symbol = symbol;
```

```
public event EventHandler PriceChanged;

protected virtual void OnPriceChanged (EventArgs e) =>
  PriceChanged?.Invoke (this, e);

public decimal Price
{
  get => price;
  set
  {
    if (price == value) return;
    price = value;
    OnPriceChanged (EventArgs.Empty);
  }
}
}
```

Note that we also used the EventArgs.Empty property—this
saves instantiating an instance of EventArgs.

Event Accessors

An event's *accessors* are the implementations of its += and -=
functions. By default, accessors are implemented implicitly by
the compiler. Consider this event declaration:

```
public event EventHandler PriceChanged;
```

The compiler converts this to the following:

- A private delegate field
- A public pair of event accessor functions, whose implementations forward the += and -= operations to the private
  delegate field

You can take over this process by defining *explicit* event accessors. Here's a manual implementation of the PriceChanged
event from our previous example:

```
EventHandler priceChanged;   // Private delegate
public event EventHandler PriceChanged
{
  add     { priceChanged += value; }
```

```
    remove { priceChanged -= value; }
  }
```

This example is functionally identical to C#'s default accessor implementation (except that C# also ensures thread safety around updating the delegate). By defining event accessors ourselves, we instruct C# not to generate default field and accessor logic.

With explicit event accessors, you can apply more complex strategies to the storage and access of the underlying delegate. This is useful when the event accessors are merely relays for another class that is broadcasting the event, or when explicitly implementing an interface that declares an event:

```
public interface IFoo { event EventHandler Ev; }
class Foo : IFoo
{
  EventHandler ev;
  event EventHandler IFoo.Ev
  {
    add { ev += value; } remove { ev -= value; }
  }
}
```

Lambda Expressions

A *lambda expression* is an unnamed method written in place of a delegate instance. The compiler immediately converts the lambda expression to either of the following:

- A delegate instance.

- An *expression tree*, of type Expression<TDelegate>, representing the code inside the lambda expression in a traversable object model. This allows the lambda expression to be interpreted later at runtime (we describe the process in Chapter 8 of C# *12 in a Nutshell*).

In the following example, x => x * x is a lambda expression:

```
Transformer sqr = x => x * x;
Console.WriteLine (sqr(3));    // 9

delegate int Transformer (int i);
```

NOTE

Internally, the compiler resolves lambda expressions of this type by writing a private method and moving the expression's code into that method.

A lambda expression has the following form:

```
(parameters) => expression-or-statement-block
```

For convenience, you can omit the parentheses if and only if there is exactly one parameter of an inferable type.

In our example, there is a single parameter, x, and the expression is x * x:

```
x => x * x;
```

Each parameter of the lambda expression corresponds to a delegate parameter, and the type of the expression (which can be void) corresponds to the return type of the delegate.

In our example, x corresponds to parameter i, and the expression x * x corresponds to the return type int, therefore making it compatible with the Transformer delegate.

A lambda expression's code can be a *statement block* instead of an expression. We can rewrite our example as follows:

```
x => { return x * x; };
```

Lambda expressions are used most commonly with the Func and Action delegates, so you will most often see our earlier expression written as follows:

```
Func<int,int> sqr = x => x * x;
```

The compiler can usually *infer* the type of lambda parameters contextually. When this is not the case, you can specify parameter types explicitly:

```
Func<int,int> sqr = (int x) => x * x;
```

Here's an example of an expression that accepts two parameters:

```
Func<string,string,int> totalLength =
  (s1, s2) => s1.Length + s2.Length;

int total = totalLength ("hello", "world");  // total=10;
```

Assuming Clicked is an event of type EventHandler, the following attaches an event handler via a lambda expression:

```
obj.Clicked += (sender,args) => Console.Write ("Click");
```

Here's an example of an expression that takes zero arguments:

```
Func<string> greeter = () => "Hello, world";
```

From C# 10, the compiler permits implicit typing with lambda expressions that can be resolved via the Func and Action delegates, so we can shorten this statement to:

```
var greeter = () => "Hello, world";
```

If the lambda expression has arguments, you must specify their types in order to use var:

```
var sqr = (int x) => x * x;
```

The compiler infers sqr to be of type Func<int,int>.

Default Lambda Parameters (C# 12)

Just as ordinary methods can have optional parameters:

```
void Print (string info = "") => Console.Write (info);
```

so, too, can lambda expressions:

```
var print = (string info = "") => Console.Write (info);

print ("Hello");
print ();
```

This feature is useful with libraries such as ASP.NET Minimal API.

Capturing Outer Variables

A lambda expression can reference any variables that are accessible where the lambda expression is defined. These are called *outer variables* and can include local variables, parameters, and fields:

```
int factor = 2;
Func<int, int> multiplier = n => n * factor;
Console.WriteLine (multiplier (3));        // 6
```

Outer variables referenced by a lambda expression are called *captured variables*. A lambda expression that captures variables is called a *closure*. Captured variables are evaluated when the delegate is actually *invoked*, not when the variables were *captured*:

```
int factor = 2;
Func<int, int> multiplier = n => n * factor;
factor = 10;
Console.WriteLine (multiplier (3));        // 30
```

Lambda expressions can themselves update captured variables:

```
int seed = 0;
Func<int> natural = () => seed++;
Console.WriteLine (natural());             // 0
Console.WriteLine (natural());             // 1
Console.WriteLine (seed);                  // 2
```

Captured variables have their lifetimes extended to that of the delegate. In the following example, the local variable seed would ordinarily disappear from scope when Natural finished executing. But because seed has been *captured*, its lifetime is extended to that of the capturing delegate, natural:

```
Func<int> natural = Natural();
Console.WriteLine (natural());             // 0
Console.WriteLine (natural());             // 1

static Func<int> Natural()
{
```

```
    int seed = 0;
    return () => seed++;        // Returns a closure
}
```

Variables can also be captured by anonymous methods and local methods. The rules for captured variables, in these cases, are the same.

Static lambdas

From C# 9, you can ensure that a lambda expression, local function, or anonymous method doesn't capture state by applying the `static` keyword. This can be useful in micro-optimization scenarios to prevent the (potentially unintentional) memory allocation and cleanup of a closure. For example, we can apply the static modifier to a lambda expression as follows:

```
Func<int, int> multiplier = static n => n * 2;
```

If we later tried to modify the lambda expression such that it captured a local variable, the compiler will generate an error. This feature is more useful in local methods (because a lambda expression itself incurs a memory allocation). In the following example, the `Multiply` method cannot access the `factor` variable:

```
void Foo()
{
    int factor = 123;
    static int Multiply (int x) => x * 2;
}
```

Applying `static` here is also arguably useful as a documentation tool, indicating a reduced level of coupling. Static lambdas can still access static variables and constants (because these do not require a closure).

Capturing iteration variables

When you capture an iteration variable in a for loop, C# treats
the iteration variable as though it were declared *outside* the
loop. This means that the *same* variable is captured in each
iteration. The following program writes 333 instead of 012:

```
Action[] actions = new Action[3];

for (int i = 0; i < 3; i++)
  actions [i] = () => Console.Write (i);

foreach (Action a in actions) a();       // 333
```

Each closure (shown in boldface) captures the same variable,
i. (This actually makes sense when you consider that i is a
variable whose value persists between loop iterations; you can
even explicitly change i within the loop body if you want.) The
consequence is that when the delegates are later invoked, each
delegate sees i's value at the time of *invocation*—which is 3.
The solution, if we want to write 012, is to assign the iteration
variable to a local variable that is scoped *within* the loop:

```
Action[] actions = new Action[3];
for (int i = 0; i < 3; i++)
{
  int loopScopedi = i;
  actions [i] = () => Console.Write (loopScopedi);
}
foreach (Action a in actions) a();       // 012
```

This causes the closure to capture a *different* variable on each
iteration.

Note that (from C# 5) the iteration variable in a foreach loop is implicitly local, so you can safely close over it without needing a temporary variable.

Lambda Expressions Versus Local Methods

The functionality of local methods (see "Local methods" on page 75) overlaps with that of lambda expressions. Local methods have the advantages of allowing for recursion and avoiding the clutter of specifying a delegate. Avoiding the indirection of a delegate also makes them slightly more efficient, and they can access local variables of the containing method without the compiler having to "hoist" the captured variables into a hidden class.

However, in many cases you *need* a delegate, most commonly when calling a higher-order function (i.e., a method with a delegate-typed parameter):

```
public void Foo (Func<int,bool> predicate) { ... }
```

In such cases, you need a delegate anyway, and it's precisely in these cases that lambda expressions are usually terser and cleaner.

Anonymous Methods

Anonymous methods are a C# 2.0 feature that has been mostly subsumed by lambda expressions. An anonymous method is like a lambda expression except that it lacks implicitly typed parameters, expression syntax (an anonymous method must always be a statement block), and the ability to compile to an expression tree. To write an anonymous method, you include the delegate keyword followed (optionally) by a parameter declaration and then a method body. For example:

```
Transformer sqr = delegate (int x) {return x * x;};
Console.WriteLine (sqr(3));        // 9

delegate int Transformer (int i);
```

The first line is semantically equivalent to the following lambda expression:

```
Transformer sqr =          (int x) => {return x * x;};
```

Or simply:

```
Transformer sqr =          x  => x * x;
```

A unique feature of anonymous methods is that you can omit the parameter declaration entirely—even if the delegate expects it. This can be useful in declaring events with a default empty handler:

```
public event EventHandler Clicked = delegate { };
```

This avoids the need for a null check before firing the event. The following is also legal (notice the lack of parameters):

```
Clicked += delegate { Console.Write ("clicked"); };
```

Anonymous methods capture outer variables in the same way lambda expressions do.

try Statements and Exceptions

A try statement specifies a code block subject to error-handling or cleanup code. The try *block* must be followed by one or more catch *blocks* and/or a finally *block*. The catch block executes when an error is thrown in the try block. The finally block executes after execution leaves the try block (or if present, the catch block) to perform cleanup code, whether or not an exception was thrown.

A catch block has access to an Exception object that contains information about the error. You use a catch block to either compensate for the error or *rethrow* the exception. You rethrow an exception if you merely want to log the problem, or if you want to rethrow a new, higher-level exception type.

A finally block adds determinism to your program by always executing no matter what. It's useful for cleanup tasks such as closing network connections.

A try statement looks like this:

```
try
{
  ... // exception may get thrown within execution of
      // this block
}
catch (ExceptionA ex)
{
  ... // handle exception of type ExceptionA
}
catch (ExceptionB ex)
{
  ... // handle exception of type ExceptionB
}
finally
{
  ... // cleanup code
}
```

Consider the following code:

```
int x = 3, y = 0;
Console.WriteLine (x / y);
```

Because y is zero, the runtime throws a DivideByZeroException and our program terminates. We can prevent this by catching the exception as follows:

```
try
{
  int x = 3, y = 0;
  Console.WriteLine (x / y);
}
catch (DivideByZeroException)
{
  Console.Write ("y cannot be zero. ");
}
// Execution resumes here after exception...
```

When an exception is thrown within a `try` statement, the CLR performs a test:

Does the `try` statement have any compatible `catch` blocks?

- If so, execution jumps to the compatible `catch` block, followed by the `finally` block (if present), and then execution continues normally.

- If not, execution jumps directly to the `finally` block (if present), and then the CLR looks up the call stack for other `try` blocks and, if found, repeats the test.

If no function in the call stack takes responsibility for the exception, an error dialog is displayed to the user and the program terminates.

The catch Clause

A `catch` clause specifies what type of exception to catch. This must be either `System.Exception` or a subclass of `System.Exception`. Catching `System.Exception` catches all possible errors. This is useful when:

- Your program can potentially recover regardless of the specific exception type.

- You plan to rethrow the exception (perhaps after logging it).

- Your error handler is the last resort, prior to termination of the program.

More typically, though, you catch *specific exception types* in order to avoid having to deal with circumstances for which your handler wasn't designed (e.g., an OutOfMemoryException).

You can handle multiple exception types with multiple catch clauses:

```
try
{
  DoSomething();
}
catch (IndexOutOfRangeException ex) { ... }
catch (FormatException ex)          { ... }
catch (OverflowException ex)        { ... }
```

Only one catch clause executes for a given exception. If you want to include a safety net to catch more general exceptions (such as System.Exception), you must put the more specific handlers *first*.

You can catch an exception without specifying a variable, if you don't need to access its properties:

```
catch (OverflowException)   // no variable
{ ... }
```

Furthermore, you can omit both the variable and the type (meaning that all exceptions will be caught):

```
catch { ... }
```

Exception filters

You can specify an *exception filter* in a catch clause by adding a when clause:

```
catch (WebException ex)
  when (ex.Status == WebExceptionStatus.Timeout)
{
  ...
}
```

If a WebException is thrown in this example, the Boolean expression following the when keyword is then evaluated. If the result is false, the catch block in question is ignored, and any subsequent catch clauses are considered. With exception filters, it can be meaningful to catch the same exception type again:

```
catch (WebException ex) when (ex.Status == something)
{ ... }
catch (WebException ex) when (ex.Status == somethingelse)
{ ... }
```

The Boolean expression in the when clause can be side-effecting, such as a method that logs the exception for diagnostic purposes.

The finally Block

A finally block always executes—whether or not an exception is thrown and whether or not the try block runs to completion. finally blocks are typically used for cleanup code.

A finally block executes either:

- After a catch block finishes
- After control leaves the try block because of a jump statement (e.g., return or goto)
- After the try block ends

A finally block helps add determinism to a program. In the following example, the file that we open *always* gets closed, regardless of whether:

- The try block finishes normally.
- Execution returns early because the file is empty (EndOf Stream).
- An IOException is thrown while the file is being read.

```
static void ReadFile()
{
  StreamReader reader = null;   // In System.IO namespace
  try
  {
    reader = File.OpenText ("file.txt");
    if (reader.EndOfStream) return;
    Console.WriteLine (reader.ReadToEnd());
  }
  finally
  {
    if (reader != null) reader.Dispose();
  }
}
```

In this example, we closed the file by calling `Dispose` on the `StreamReader`. Calling `Dispose` on an object, within a `finally` block, is a standard convention throughout .NET and is supported explicitly in C# through the `using` statement.

The using statement

Many classes encapsulate unmanaged resources such as file handles, graphics handles, or database connections. These classes implement `System.IDisposable`, which defines a single parameterless method named `Dispose` to clean up these resources. The `using` statement provides an elegant syntax for calling `Dispose` on an `IDisposable` object within a `finally` block.

The following:

```
using (StreamReader reader = File.OpenText ("file.txt"))
{
  ...
}
```

is precisely equivalent to:

```
{
  StreamReader reader = File.OpenText ("file.txt");
  try
  {
    ...
  }
```

```
  finally
  {
    if (reader != null) ((IDisposable)reader).Dispose();
  }
}
```

using declarations

If you omit the brackets and statement block following a using statement, it becomes a *using declaration* (C# 8+). The resource is then disposed when execution falls outside the *enclosing* statement block:

```
if (File.Exists ("file.txt"))
{
  using var reader = File.OpenText ("file.txt");
  Console.WriteLine (reader.ReadLine());
  ...
}
```

In this case, reader will be disposed when execution falls outside the if statement block.

Throwing Exceptions

Exceptions can be thrown either by the runtime or in user code. In this example, Display throws a System.ArgumentNull Exception:

```
static void Display (string name)
{
  if (name == null)
    throw new ArgumentNullException (nameof (name));

  Console.WriteLine (name);
}
```

throw expressions

From C# 7, throw can appear as an expression in expression-bodied functions:

```
public string Foo() => throw new NotImplementedException();
```

A throw expression can also appear in a ternary conditional expression:

```
string ProperCase (string value) =>
  value == null ? throw new ArgumentException ("value") :
  value == "" ? "" :
  char.ToUpper (value[0]) + value.Substring (1);
```

Rethrowing an exception

You can capture and rethrow an exception as follows:

```
try {  ...  }
catch (Exception ex)
{
  // Log error
  ...
  throw;          // Rethrow same exception
}
```

Rethrowing in this manner lets you log an error without *swallowing* it. It also lets you back out of handling an exception should circumstances turn out to be outside what you expected.

NOTE

If we replaced throw with throw ex, the example would still work, but the StackTrace property of the exception would no longer reflect the original error.

The other common scenario is to rethrow a more specific or meaningful exception type:

```
try
{
  ... // parse a date of birth from XML element data
}
catch (FormatException ex)
{
  throw new XmlException ("Invalid date of birth", ex);
}
```

When rethrowing a different exception, you can populate the
InnerException property with the original exception to aid
debugging. Nearly all types of exceptions provide a constructor
for this purpose (such as in our example).

Key Properties of System.Exception

The most important properties of System.Exception are the
following:

StackTrace

> A string representing all the methods that are called from
> the origin of the exception to the catch block.

Message

> A string with a description of the error.

InnerException

> The inner exception (if any) that caused the outer excep-
> tion. This, itself, might have another InnerException.

Enumeration and Iterators

Enumeration

An *enumerator* is a read-only, forward-only cursor over a
sequence of values. C# treats a type as an enumerator if it does
any of the following:

- Has a public parameterless method named MoveNext and
  property called Current

- Implements System.Collections.Generic.IEnumerator<T>

- Implements System.Collections.IEnumerator

The foreach statement iterates over an *enumerable* object. An
enumerable object is the logical representation of a sequence.
It is not itself a cursor but an object that produces cursors
over itself. C# treats a type as enumerable if it does any of the
following (the check is performed in this order):

- Has a public parameterless method named `GetEnumerator` that returns an enumerator

- Implements `System.Collections.Generic.IEnumerable<T>`

- Implements `System.Collections.IEnumerable`

- (From C# 9) Can bind to an *extension method* named `GetEnumerator` that returns an enumerator (see "Extension Methods" on page 174)

The enumeration pattern is as follows:

```
class Enumerator    // Typically implements IEnumerator<T>
{
  public IteratorVariableType Current { get {...} }
  public bool MoveNext() {...}
}
class Enumerable    // Typically implements IEnumerable<T>
{
  public Enumerator GetEnumerator() {...}
}
```

Here is the high-level way to iterate through the characters in the word *beer* using a `foreach` statement:

```
foreach (char c in "beer") Console.WriteLine (c);
```

Here is the low-level way to iterate through the characters in *beer* without using a `foreach` statement:

```
using (var enumerator = "beer".GetEnumerator())
  while (enumerator.MoveNext())
  {
    var element = enumerator.Current;
    Console.WriteLine (element);
  }
```

If the enumerator implements `IDisposable`, the `foreach` statement also acts as a `using` statement, implicitly disposing the enumerator object.

Collection Initializers and Collection Expressions

You can instantiate and populate an enumerable object in a single step. For example:

```
using System.Collections.Generic;

List<int> list = new List<int> {1, 2, 3};
```

From C# 12, you can shorten the last line further with a *collection expression* (note the square brackets):

```
List<int> list = [1, 2, 3];
```

NOTE

Collection expressions are *target-typed*, meaning that the type of [1,2,3] depends on the type to which it's assigned (in this case, List<int>). In the following example, the target type is an array:

```
int[] array = [1, 2, 3];
```

Target typing means that you can omit the type in other scenarios where the compiler can infer it, such as when calling methods:

```
Foo ([1, 2, 3]);
void Foo (List<int> numbers) { ... }
```

The compiler translates this into the following:

```
List<int> list = new List<int>();
list.Add (1); list.Add (2); list.Add (3);
```

This requires that the enumerable object implements the Sys tem.Collections.IEnumerable interface and that it has an Add method that has the appropriate number of parameters for the call. You can similarly initialize dictionaries (types that implement System.Collections.IDictionary) as follows:

```
var dict = new Dictionary<int, string>()
{
  { 5, "five" },
  { 10, "ten" }
};
```

Or, more succinctly:

```
var dict = new Dictionary<int, string>()
{
  [5] = "five",
  [10] = "ten"
};
```

The latter is valid not only with dictionaries but with any type for which an indexer exists.

Iterators

Whereas a `foreach` statement is a *consumer* of an enumerator, an iterator is a *producer* of an enumerator. In this example, we use an iterator to return a sequence of Fibonacci numbers (for which each number is the sum of the previous two):

```
foreach (int fib in Fibs (6))
  Console.Write (fib + "  ");

IEnumerable<int> Fibs (int fibCount)
{
  for (int i=0, prevFib=1, curFib=1; i<fibCount; i++)
  {
    yield return prevFib;
    int newFib = prevFib+curFib;
    prevFib = curFib;
    curFib = newFib;
  }
}
OUTPUT: 1  1  2  3  5  8
```

Whereas a `return` statement expresses, "Here's the value you asked me to return from this method," a `yield return` statement expresses, "Here's the next element you asked me to yield from this enumerator." On each `yield` statement, control is returned to the caller, but the callee's state is maintained so that the method can continue executing as soon as the caller enumerates the next element. The lifetime of this state is bound to the enumerator, such that the state can be released when the caller has finished enumerating.

NOTE

The compiler converts iterator methods into private classes that implement IEnumerable<T> and/or IEnumerator<T>. The logic within the iterator block is "inverted" and spliced into the MoveNext method and the Current property on the compiler-written enumerator class, which effectively becomes a state machine. This means that when you call an iterator method, all you're doing is instantiating the compiler-written class; none of your code actually runs! Your code runs only when you start enumerating over the resultant sequence, typically with a foreach statement.

Iterator Semantics

An iterator is a method, property, or indexer that contains one or more yield statements. An iterator must return one of the following four interfaces (otherwise, the compiler will generate an error):

```
System.Collections.IEnumerable
System.Collections.IEnumerator
System.Collections.Generic.IEnumerable<T>
System.Collections.Generic.IEnumerator<T>
```

Iterators that return an *enumerator* interface tend to be used less often. They're useful when you're writing a custom collection class: typically, you name the iterator GetEnumerator and have your class implement IEnumerable<T>.

Iterators that return an *enumerable* interface are more common—and simpler to use because you don't need to write a collection class. The compiler, behind the scenes, writes a private class implementing IEnumerable<T> (as well as IEnumerator<T>).

Multiple yield statements

An iterator can include multiple yield statements:

```
foreach (string s in Foo())
  Console.Write (s + " ");    // One Two Three

IEnumerable<string> Foo()
{
  yield return "One";
  yield return "Two";
  yield return "Three";
}
```

yield break

A return statement is illegal in an iterator block; instead, you must use the yield break statement to indicate that the iterator block should exit early, without returning more elements. We can modify Foo as follows to demonstrate:

```
IEnumerable<string> Foo (bool breakEarly)
{
  yield return "One";
  yield return "Two";
  if (breakEarly) yield break;
  yield return "Three";
}
```

Composing Sequences

Iterators are highly composable. We can extend our Fibonacci example by adding the following method to the class:

```
Enumerable<int> EvenNumbersOnly (
  IEnumerable<int> sequence)
  {
    foreach (int x in sequence)
      if ((x % 2) == 0)
        yield return x;
  }
}
```

We can then output even Fibonacci numbers as follows:

```
foreach (int fib in EvenNumbersOnly (Fibs (6)))
  Console.Write (fib + " ");   // 2 8
```

Each element is not calculated until the last moment—when requested by a `MoveNext()` operation. Figure 5 shows the data requests and data output over time.

Figure 5. Composing sequences

The composability of the iterator pattern is essential in building LINQ queries.

Nullable Value Types

Reference types can represent a nonexistent value with a null reference. Value types, however, cannot ordinarily represent null values. For example:

```
string s = null;    // OK - reference type
int i = null;       // Compile error - int cannot be null
```

To represent null in a value type, you must use a special construct called a *nullable type*. A nullable type is denoted with a value type followed by the ? symbol:

```
int? i = null;                      // OK - nullable type
Console.WriteLine (i == null);      // True
```

Nullable<T> Struct

T? translates into System.Nullable<T>. Nullable<T> is a light-weight immutable structure, having only two fields, to represent Value and HasValue. The essence of System.Nullable<T> is very simple:

```
public struct Nullable<T> where T : struct
{
  public T Value {get;}
  public bool HasValue {get;}
  public T GetValueOrDefault();
  public T GetValueOrDefault (T defaultValue);
  ...
}
```

The following code:

```
int? i = null;
Console.WriteLine (i == null);              // True
```

translates to:

```
Nullable<int> i = new Nullable<int>();
Console.WriteLine (! i.HasValue);           // True
```

Attempting to retrieve Value when HasValue is false throws an InvalidOperationException. GetValueOrDefault() returns Value if HasValue is true; otherwise, it returns new T() or a specified custom default value.

The default value of T? is null.

Nullable Conversions

The conversion from T to T? is implicit, while from T? to T the conversion is explicit. For example:

```
int? x = 5;       // implicit
int y = (int)x;   // explicit
```

The explicit cast is directly equivalent to calling the nullable object's Value property. Hence, an InvalidOperationException is thrown if HasValue is false.

Boxing/Unboxing Nullable Values

When T? is boxed, the boxed value on the heap contains T, not T?. This optimization is possible because a boxed value is a reference type that can already express null.

C# also permits the unboxing of nullable types with the as operator. The result will be null if the cast fails:

```
object o = "string";
int? x = o as int?;
Console.WriteLine (x.HasValue);   // False
```

Operator Lifting

The Nullable<T> struct does not define operators such as <, >, or even ==. Despite this, the following code compiles and executes correctly:

```
int? x = 5;
int? y = 10;
bool b = x < y;   // true
```

This works because the compiler borrows or "lifts" the less-than operator from the underlying value type. Semantically, it translates the preceding comparison expression into this:

```
bool b = (x.HasValue && y.HasValue)
         ? (x.Value < y.Value)
         : false;
```

In other words, if both x and y have values, it compares via int's less-than operator; otherwise, it returns false.

Operator lifting means that you can implicitly use T's operators on T?. You can define operators for T? in order to provide special-purpose null behavior, but in the vast majority of cases, it's best to rely on the compiler automatically applying systematic nullable logic for you.

The compiler performs null logic differently depending on the category of operator.

Equality operators (==, !=)

Lifted equality operators handle nulls just like reference types do. This means two null values are equal:

```
Console.WriteLine (        null ==        null);  // True
Console.WriteLine ((bool?)null == (bool?)null);  // True
```

Further:

- If exactly one operand is null, the operands are unequal.
- If both operands are non-null, their Values are compared.

Relational operators (<, <=, >=, >)

The relational operators work on the principle that it is meaningless to compare null operands. This means that comparing a null value to either a null or a non-null value returns false:

```
bool b = x < y;    // Translation:

bool b = (x == null || y == null)
  ? false
  : (x.Value < y.Value);

// b is false (assuming x is 5 and y is null)
```

All other operators (+, −, *, /, %, &, |, ^, <<, >>, +, ++, --, !, ~)

These operators return null when any of the operands are null. This pattern should be familiar to SQL users:

```
int? c = x + y;    // Translation:

int? c = (x == null || y == null)
         ? null
         : (int?) (x.Value + y.Value);

// c is null (assuming x is 5 and y is null)
```

An exception is when the & and | operators are applied to
bool?, which we will discuss shortly.

Mixing nullable and non-nullable types

You can mix and match nullable and non-nullable types (this
works because there is an implicit conversion from T to T?):

```
int? a = null;
int b = 2;
int? c = a + b;   // c is null - equivalent to a + (int?)b
```

bool? with & and | Operators

When supplied operands of type bool?, the & and | operators
treat null as an *unknown value*. So, null | true is true,
because:

- If the unknown value is false, the result would be true.
- If the unknown value is true, the result would be true.

Similarly, null & false is false. This behavior should be familiar to SQL users. The following example enumerates other
combinations:

```
bool? n = null, f = false, t = true;
Console.WriteLine (n | n);    // (null)
Console.WriteLine (n | f);    // (null)
Console.WriteLine (n | t);    // True
Console.WriteLine (n & n);    // (null)
Console.WriteLine (n & f);    // False
Console.WriteLine (n & t);    // (null)
```

Nullable Types and Null Operators

Nullable types work particularly well with the ?? operator (see "Null-Coalescing Operator" on page 56). For example:

```
int? x = null;
int y = x ?? 5;        // y is 5

int? a = null, b = null, c = 123;
Console.WriteLine (a ?? b ?? c);  // 123
```

Using ?? on a nullable value type is equivalent to calling Get ValueOrDefault with an explicit default value, except that the expression for the default value is never evaluated if the variable is not null.

Nullable types also work well with the null-conditional operator (see "Null-Conditional Operator" on page 57). In the following example, length evaluates to null:

```
System.Text.StringBuilder sb = null;
int? length = sb?.ToString().Length;
```

We can combine this with the null-coalescing operator to evaluate to zero instead of null:

```
int length = sb?.ToString().Length ?? 0;
```

Nullable Reference Types

Whereas *nullable value types* bring nullability to value types, *nullable reference types* (from C# 8) do the opposite. When enabled, they bring (a degree of) *non-nullability* to reference types, with the purpose of helping to avoid NullReference Exceptions.

Nullable reference types introduce a level of safety that's enforced purely by the compiler in the form of warnings when it detects code that's at risk of generating a NullReference Exception.

To enable nullable reference types, you must either add the `Nullable` element to your *.csproj* project file (if you want to enable it for the entire project):

```
<Nullable>enable</Nullable>
```

and/or you can use the following directives in your code, in the places where it should take effect:

```
#nullable enable    // enables NRT from this point on
#nullable disable   // disables NRT from this point on
#nullable restore   // resets NRT to project setting
```

After it is enabled, the compiler makes non-nullability the default: if you want a reference type to accept nulls without the compiler generating a warning, you must apply the ? suffix to indicate a *nullable reference type*. In the following example, `s1` is non-nullable, whereas `s2` is nullable:

```
#nullable enable    // Enable nullable reference types

string s1 = null;   // Generates a compiler warning!
string? s2 = null;  // OK: s2 is nullable reference type
```

NOTE

Because nullable reference types are compile-time constructs, there's no runtime difference between `string` and `string?`. In contrast, nullable value types introduce something concrete into the type system—namely, the `Nullable<T>` struct.

The following also generates a warning because `x` is not initialized:

```
class Foo { string x; }
```

The warning disappears if you initialize `x`, either via a field initializer or via code in the constructor.

The compiler also warns you upon dereferencing a nullable reference type if it thinks a `NullReferenceException` might occur. In the following example, accessing the string's `Length` property generates a warning:

```
void Foo (string? s) => Console.Write (s.Length);
```

To remove the warning, you can use the *null-forgiving operator* (`!`):

```
void Foo (string? s) => Console.Write (s!.Length);
```

Our use of the null-forgiving operator in this example is dangerous in that we could end up throwing the very `NullReferenceException` we were trying to avoid in the first place. We could fix it as follows:

```
void Foo (string? s)
{
  if (s != null) Console.Write (s.Length);
}
```

Notice now that we don't need the null-forgiving operator. This is because the compiler performs static analysis and is smart enough to infer—at least in simple cases—when a dereference is safe and there's no chance of a `NullReferenceException`.

The compiler's ability to detect and warn is not bulletproof, and there are also limits to what's possible in terms of coverage. For instance, it's unable to know whether an array's elements have been populated, and so the following does not generate a warning:

```
var strings = new string[10];
Console.WriteLine (strings[0].Length);
```

Extension Methods

Extension methods allow an existing type to be extended with new methods without altering the definition of the original type. An extension method is a static method of a static class, where the `this` modifier is applied to the first parameter. The type of the first parameter will be the type that is extended. For example:

```
public static class StringHelper
{
  public static bool IsCapitalized (this string s)
  {
    if (string.IsNullOrEmpty (s)) return false;
    return char.IsUpper (s[0]);
  }
}
```

The IsCapitalized extension method can be called as though it were an instance method on a string, as follows:

```
Console.Write ("Perth".IsCapitalized());
```

An extension method call, when compiled, is translated back into an ordinary static method call:

```
Console.Write (StringHelper.IsCapitalized ("Perth"));
```

Interfaces can be extended, too:

```
public static T First<T> (this IEnumerable<T> sequence)
{
  foreach (T element in sequence)
    return element;
  throw new InvalidOperationException ("No elements!");
}
...
Console.WriteLine ("Seattle".First());   // S
```

Extension Method Chaining

Extension methods, like instance methods, provide a tidy way to chain functions. Consider the following two functions:

```
public static class StringHelper
{
  public static string Pluralize (this string s) {...}
  public static string Capitalize (this string s) {...}
}
```

x and y are equivalent, and both evaluate to "Sausages", but x uses extension methods, whereas y uses static methods:

```
string x = "sausage".Pluralize().Capitalize();

string y = StringHelper.Capitalize
            (StringHelper.Pluralize ("sausage"));
```

Ambiguity and Resolution

Any compatible instance method will always take precedence over an extension method—even when the extension method's parameters are more specifically type-matched.

If two extension methods have the same signature, the extension method must be called as an ordinary static method to disambiguate the method to call. If one extension method has more specific arguments, however, the more specific method takes precedence.

Anonymous Types

An *anonymous type* is a simple class created on the fly to store a set of values. To create an anonymous type, you use the new keyword followed by an object initializer, specifying the properties and values the type will contain. For example:

```
var dude = new { Name = "Bob", Age = 1 };
```

The compiler resolves this by writing a private nested type with read-only properties for Name (type string) and Age (type int). You must use the var keyword to reference an anonymous type, because the type's name is compiler-generated.

The property name of an anonymous type can be inferred from an expression that is itself an identifier; consider, for example:

```
int Age = 1;
var dude = new { Name = "Bob", Age };
```

This is equivalent to:

```
var dude = new { Name = "Bob", Age = Age };
```

You can create arrays of anonymous types as follows:

```
var dudes = new[]
{
  new { Name = "Bob", Age = 30 },
  new { Name = "Mary", Age = 40 }
};
```

Anonymous types are used primarily when you're writing LINQ queries.

Anonymous types are immutable, so instances cannot be modified after creation. However, from C# 10, you can use the with keyword to create a copy with variations, as you would with records. See "Nondestructive Mutation" on page 183 for an example.

Tuples

Like anonymous types, *tuples* (C# 7+) provide a simple way to store a set of values. Tuples were introduced into C# with the main purpose of allowing methods to return multiple values without resorting to out parameters (something you cannot do with anonymous types). Since then, however, *records* have been introduced, offering a concise typed approach that we will describe in the following section.

The simplest way to create a *tuple literal* is to list the desired values in parentheses. This creates a tuple with *unnamed* elements:

```
var bob = ("Bob", 23);
Console.WriteLine (bob.Item1);   // Bob
Console.WriteLine (bob.Item2);   // 23
```

Unlike with anonymous types, var is optional, and you can specify a *tuple type* explicitly:

```
(string,int) bob  = ("Bob", 23);
```

This means that you can usefully return a tuple from a method:

```
(string,int) person = GetPerson();
Console.WriteLine (person.Item1);   // Bob
Console.WriteLine (person.Item2);   // 23
```

```
(string,int) GetPerson() => ("Bob", 23);
```

Tuples play well with generics, so the following types are all legal:

```
Task<(string,int)>
Dictionary<(string,int),Uri>
IEnumerable<(int ID, string Name)>   // See below...
```

Tuples are *value types* with *mutable* (read/write) elements. This means that you can modify Item1, Item2, and so on, after creating a tuple.

Naming Tuple Elements

You can optionally give meaningful names to elements when creating tuple literals:

```
var tuple = (Name:"Bob", Age:23);
Console.WriteLine (tuple.Name);     // Bob
Console.WriteLine (tuple.Age);      // 23
```

You can do the same when specifying *tuple types*:

```
static (string Name, int Age) GetPerson() => ("Bob",23);
```

Element names are automatically *inferred* from property or field names:

```
var now = DateTime.Now;
var tuple = (now.Day, now.Month, now.Year);
Console.WriteLine (tuple.Day);                  // OK
```

NOTE

Tuples are syntactic sugar for using a family of generic structs called ValueTuple<T1> and ValueTuple<T1,T2>, which have fields named Item1, Item2, and so on. Hence (string,int) is an alias for ValueTuple<string,int>. This means that "named elements" exist only in the source code—and the imagination of the compiler—and mostly disappear at runtime.

Deconstructing Tuples

Tuples implicitly support the deconstruction pattern (see "Deconstructors" on page 78), so you can easily *deconstruct* a tuple into individual variables. Consider the following:

```
var bob = ("Bob", 23);
string name = bob.Item1;
int age = bob.Item2;
```

With the tuple's deconstructor, you can simplify the code to this:

```
var bob = ("Bob", 23);
(string name, int age) = bob;    // Deconstruct bob into
                                 // name and age.
Console.WriteLine (name);
Console.WriteLine (age);
```

The syntax for deconstruction is confusingly similar to the syntax for declaring a tuple with named elements! The following highlights the difference:

```
(string name, int age)      = bob;  // Deconstructing
(string name, int age) bob2 = bob;  // Declaring tuple
```

Records

A *record* (from C# 9) is a special kind of class or struct that's designed to work well with immutable (read-only) data. Its most useful feature is allowing *nondestructive mutation*, whereby to "modify" an immutable object, you create a new one and copy over the data while incorporating your modifications.

Records are also useful in creating types that just combine or hold data. In simple cases, they eliminate boilerplate code while honoring *structural equality* semantics (two objects are the same if their data is the same), which is usually what you want with immutable types.

A record is purely a C# compile-time construct. At runtime, the CLR sees them just as classes or structs (with a bunch of extra "synthesized" members added by the compiler).

Defining a Record

A record definition is like a class or struct definition and can contain the same kinds of members, including fields, properties, methods, and so on. Records can implement interfaces, and (class-based) records can subclass other (class-based) records.

By default, the underlying type of a record is a class:

```
record Point { }          // Point is a class
```

From C# 10, the underlying type of a record can also be a struct:

```
record struct Point { }   // Point is a struct
```

(record class is also legal and has the same meaning as record.)

A simple record might contain just a bunch of init-only properties, and perhaps a constructor:

```
record Point
{
  public Point (double x, double y) => (X, Y) = (x, y);

  public double X { get; init; }
  public double Y { get; init; }
}
```

Upon compilation, C# transforms the record definition into a class (or struct) and performs the following additional steps:

- It writes a protected *copy constructor* (and a hidden *Clone* method) to facilitate nondestructive mutation.

- It overrides/overloads the equality-related functions to implement structural equality.

- It overrides the ToString() method (to expand the record's public properties, as with anonymous types).

The preceding record declaration expands into something like this:

```
class Point
{
  public Point (double x, double y) => (X, Y) = (x, y);

  public double X { get; init; }
  public double Y { get; init; }

  protected Point (Point original) // "Copy constructor"
  {
    this.X = original.X; this.Y = original.Y
  }

  // This method has a strange compiler-generated name:
  public virtual Point <Clone>$() => new Point (this);

  // Additional code to override Equals, ==, !=,
  // GetHashCode, ToString()...
}
```

Parameter lists

A record definition can be shortened through the use of a *parameter list*:

```
record Point (double X, double Y)
{
  ...
}
```

Parameters can include the in and params modifiers but not out or ref. If a parameter list is specified, the compiler performs the following extra steps:

- It writes an init-only property per parameter (or a writable property, in the case of record structs).
- It writes a *primary constructor* to populate the properties.

- It writes a deconstructor.

This means that we can declare our `Point` record simply as follows:

```
record Point (double X, double Y);
```

The compiler will end up generating (almost) exactly what we listed in the preceding expansion. A minor difference is that the parameter names in the primary constructor will end up as X and Y instead of x and y:

```
public Point (double X, double Y)
{
  this.X = X; this.Y = Y;
}
```

NOTE

Also, due to being a *primary constructor*, the parameters X and Y become magically available to any field or property initializers in your record. We discuss the subtleties of this later in "Primary Constructors" on page 184.

Another difference when you define a parameter list is that the compiler also generates a deconstructor:

```
public void Deconstruct (out double X, out double Y)
{
  X = this.X; Y = this.Y;
}
```

Records with parameter lists can be subclassed using the following syntax:

```
record Point3D (double X, double Y, double Z)
  : Point (X, Y);
```

The compiler then emits a primary constructor as follows:

```
class Point3D : Point
{
  public double Z { get; init; }
```

```
    public Point3D (double X, double Y, double Z)
      : base (X, Y)
      => this.Z = Z;
}
```

NOTE

Parameter lists offer a nice shortcut when you need a
class that simply groups together a bunch of values (a
product type in functional programming), and can also be
useful for prototyping. They're not so helpful when you
need to add logic to the `init` accessors (such as argument
validation).

Nondestructive Mutation

The most important step that the compiler performs with all
records is to write a *copy constructor* (and a hidden *Clone*
method). This enables nondestructive mutation via the `with`
keyword:

```
Point p1 = new Point (3, 3);
Point p2 = p1 with { Y = 4 };
Console.WriteLine (p2);        // Point { X = 3, Y = 4 }

record Point (double X, double Y);
```

In this example, p2 is a copy of p1 but with its Y property set to
4. The benefit is greater when there are more properties.

Nondestructive mutation occurs in two phases:

1. First, the *copy constructor* clones the record. By default,
   it copies each of the record's underlying fields, creating a
   faithful replica while bypassing (the overhead of) any logic
   in the `init` accessors. All fields are included (public and
   private, as well as the hidden fields that back automatic
   properties).

2. Then, each property in the *member initializer list* is updated (this time using the `init` accessors).

The compiler translates the following:

```
Test t2 = t1 with { A = 10, C = 30 };
```

into something functionally equivalent to this:

```
Test t2 = new Test(t1);   // Clone t1
t2.A = 10;                 // Update property A
t2.C = 30;                 // Update property C
```

(The same code would not compile if you wrote it explicitly because A and C are init-only properties. Furthermore, the copy constructor is *protected*; C# works around this by invoking it via a public hidden method that it writes into the record called `<Clone>$`.)

If necessary, you can define your own *copy constructor*. C# will then use your definition instead of writing one itself:

```
protected Point (Point original)
{
  this.X = original.X; this.Y = original.Y;
}
```

When subclassing another record, the copy constructor is responsible for copying only its own fields. To copy the base record's fields, delegate to the base:

```
protected Point (Point original) : base (original)
{
  ...
}
```

Primary Constructors

When you define a record with a parameter list, the compiler generates property declarations automatically, as well as a *primary constructor* (and a deconstructor). This works well in simple cases, and in more complex cases you can omit the parameter list and write the property declarations and constructor manually. C# also offers the mildly useful intermediate option of defining a parameter list while writing some or all of the property declarations yourself:

```
record Student(int ID, string Surname, string FirstName)
{
  public int ID { get; } = ID;
}
```

In this case, we "took over" the ID property definition, defining it as read-only (instead of init-only), preventing it from partaking in nondestructive mutation. If you never need to nondestructively mutate a particular property, making it read-only lets you cache computed data in the record without having to code up a refresh mechanism.

Notice that we needed to include a *property initializer* (in boldface):

```
public int ID { get; } = ID;
```

When you "take over" a property declaration, you become responsible for initializing its value; the primary constructor no longer does this automatically. (This exactly matches the behavior when defining primary constructors on classes or structs.) Note that the ID in boldface refers to the *primary constructor parameter*, not the ID property.

In keeping with the semantics of primary constructors on classes and structs, the primary constructor parameters (ID, Surname, and FirstName in this case) are magically visible to all field and property initializers.

You can also take over a property definition with explicit accessors:

```
int _id = ID;
public int ID { get => _id; init => _id = value; }
```

Again, the ID in boldface refers to the primary constructor parameter, not the property. (The reason for there not being an ambiguity is that it's illegal to access properties from initializers.)

The fact that we must initialize the _id property with ID makes this "takeover" less useful, in that any logic in the init accessor (such as validation) will get bypassed by the primary constructor.

Records and Equality Comparison

Just as with structs, anonymous types, and tuples, records provide structural equality out of the box, meaning that two records are equal if their fields (and automatic properties) are equal:

```
var p1 = new Point (1, 2);
var p2 = new Point (1, 2);
Console.WriteLine (p1.Equals (p2));   // True

record Point (double X, double Y);
```

The *equality operator* also works with records (as it does with tuples):

```
Console.WriteLine (p1 == p2);          // True
```

Unlike with classes and structs, you do not (and cannot) override the object.Equals method if you want to customize equality behavior. Instead, you define a public Equals method with the following signature:

```
record Point (double X, double Y)
{
  public virtual bool Equals (Point other) =>
    other != null && X == other.X && Y == other.Y;
}
```

The Equals method must be virtual (not override), and it must be *strongly typed* such that it accepts the actual record type (Point in this case, not object). Once you get the signature right, the compiler will automatically patch in your method.

As with any type, if you take over equality comparison, you should also override GetHashCode(). A nice feature of records is that you don't overload != or ==; nor do you implement

`IEquatable<T>`: this is all done for you. We cover this topic fully in "Equality Comparison" in Chapter 6 of *C# 12 in a Nutshell*.

Patterns

Earlier, we demonstrated how to use the `is` operator to test whether a reference conversion will succeed, and then use its converted value:

```
if (obj is string s)
  Console.WriteLine (s.Length);
```

This employs one kind of pattern called a *type pattern*. The `is` operator also supports other patterns that were introduced in recent versions of C#. Patterns are supported in the following contexts:

- After the `is` operator (*variable* is *pattern*)
- In switch statements
- In switch expressions

We've already covered the type pattern in "Switching on types" on page 62 and "The is operator" on page 98. In this section, we cover more advanced patterns that were introduced in recent versions of C#.

Some of the more specialized patterns are intended for use in switch statements/expressions. Here, they reduce the need for `when` clauses and let you use switches where you couldn't previously.

var Pattern

The *var pattern* is a variation of the *type pattern* whereby you replace the type name with the `var` keyword. The conversion always succeeds, so its purpose is merely to let you reuse the variable that follows:

```
bool IsJanetOrJohn (string name) =>
  name.ToUpper() is var upper &&
  (upper == "JANET" || upper == "JOHN");
```

This is equivalent to:

```
bool IsJanetOrJohn (string name)
{
  string upper = name.ToUpper();
  return upper == "JANET" || upper == "JOHN";
}
```

Constant Pattern

The *constant pattern* lets you match directly to a constant and is useful when working with the object type:

```
void Foo (object obj)
{
  if (obj is 3) ...
}
```

This expression in boldface is equivalent to the following:

```
obj is int && (int)obj == 3
```

As we'll see soon, the constant pattern can become more useful with *pattern combinators*.

Relational Patterns

From C# 9, you can use the <, >, <=, and >= operators in patterns:

```
if (x is > 100) Console.Write ("x is greater than 100");
```

This becomes meaningfully useful in a switch:

```
string GetWeightCategory (decimal bmi) => bmi switch
{
  < 18.5m => "underweight",
  < 25m => "normal",
  < 30m => "overweight",
  _ => "obese"
};
```

Pattern Combinators

From C# 9, you can use the and, or, and not keywords to combine patterns:

```
bool IsJanetOrJohn (string name)
  => name.ToUpper() is "JANET" or "JOHN";

bool IsVowel (char c)
  => c is 'a' or 'e' or 'i' or 'o' or 'u';

bool Between1And9 (int n) => n is >= 1 and <= 9;

bool IsLetter (char c) => c is >= 'a' and <= 'z'
                            or >= 'A' and <= 'Z';
```

As with the && and || operators, and has higher precedence than or. You can override this with parentheses. A nice trick is to combine the not combinator with the *type pattern* to test whether an object is (not) a type:

```
if (obj is not string) ...
```

This looks nicer than:

```
if (!(obj is string)) ...
```

Tuple and Positional Patterns

The *tuple pattern* (introduced in C# 8) matches tuples:

```
var p = (2, 3);
Console.WriteLine (p is (2, 3));   // True
```

The tuple pattern can be considered a special case of the *positional pattern* (C# 8+), which matches any type that exposes a Deconstruct method (see "Deconstructors" on page 78). In the following example, we leverage the Point record's compiler-generated deconstructor:

```
var p = new Point (2, 2);
Console.WriteLine (p is (2, 2));  // True

record Point (int X, int Y);
```

You can deconstruct as you match, using the following syntax:

```
Console.WriteLine (p is (var x, var y) && x == y);
```

Here's a switch expression that combines a type pattern with a positional pattern:

```
string Print (object obj) => obj switch
{
  Point (0, 0)                    => "Empty point",
  Point (var x, var y) when x == y => "Diagonal"
  ...
};
```

Property Patterns

A *property pattern* (C# 8+) matches on one or more of an object's property values:

```
if (obj is string { Length:4 }) ...
```

However, this doesn't save much over the following:

```
if (obj is string s && s.Length == 4) ...
```

With switch statements and expressions, property patterns are more useful. Consider the System.Uri class, which represents a URI. It has properties that include Scheme, Host, Port, and IsLoopback. In writing a firewall, we could decide whether to allow or block a URI by employing a switch expression that uses property patterns:

```
bool ShouldAllow (Uri uri) => uri switch
{
  { Scheme: "http",  Port: 80  } => true,
  { Scheme: "https", Port: 443 } => true,
  { Scheme: "ftp",   Port: 21  } => true,
  { IsLoopback: true            } => true,
  _ => false
};
```

You can nest properties, making the following clause legal:

```
{ Scheme: { Length: 4 }, Port: 80 } => true,
```

which, from C# 10, can be simplified to:

```
{ Scheme.Length: 4, Port: 80 } => true,
```

You can use other patterns inside property patterns, including the relational pattern:

```
{ Host: { Length: < 1000 }, Port: > 0 } => true,
```

You can introduce a variable at the end of a clause and then consume that variable in a when clause:

```
{ Scheme: "http", Port: 80 } httpUri
    when httpUri.Host.Length < 1000 => true,
```

You can also introduce variables at the *property* level:

```
{ Scheme: "http", Port: 80, Host: var host }
    when host.Length < 1000 => true,
```

In this case, however, the following is shorter and simpler:

```
{ Scheme: "http", Port: 80, Host: { Length: < 1000 } }
```

List Patterns

List patterns (from C# 11) work with any collection type that is countable (with a Count or Length property) and indexable (with an indexer of type int or System.Index).

A list pattern matches a series of elements in square brackets:

```
int[] numbers = { 0, 1, 2, 3, 4 };
Console.Write (numbers is [0, 1, 2, 3, 4]);   // True
```

An underscore matches a single element of any value:

```
Console.Write (numbers is [0, 1, _, _, 4]);   // True
```

The var pattern also works in matching a single element:

```
Console.Write (numbers is [0, 1, var x, 3, 4] && x > 1);
```

Two dots indicate a *slice*. A slice matches zero or more elements:

```
Console.Write (numbers is [0, .., 4]);   // True
```

With arrays and other types that support indices and ranges (see "Indices and Ranges" on page 36), you can follow a slice with a var pattern:

```
Console.Write (numbers is [0, .. var mid, 4]
                  && mid.Contains (2));          // True
```

A list pattern can include at most one slice.

LINQ

LINQ, or Language Integrated Query, allows you to write struc-
tured type-safe queries over local object collections and remote
data sources. LINQ lets you query any collection implementing
IEnumerable<>, whether an array, list, XML DOM, or remote
data source (such as a table in SQL Server). LINQ offers
the benefits of both compile-time type checking and dynamic
query composition.

NOTE

A good way to experiment with LINQ is to download
LINQPad (*http://www.linqpad.net*). LINQPad lets you
interactively query local collections and SQL databases in
LINQ without any setup and is preloaded with numerous
examples.

LINQ Fundamentals

The basic units of data in LINQ are *sequences* and *elements*. A
sequence is any object that implements the generic IEnumerable
interface, and an element is each item in the sequence. In the
following example, names is a sequence, and Tom, Dick, and
Harry are elements:

```
string[] names = { "Tom", "Dick", "Harry" };
```

We call a sequence such as this a *local sequence* because it
represents a local collection of objects in memory.

A *query operator* is a method that transforms a sequence. A
typical query operator accepts an *input sequence* and emits
a transformed *output sequence*. In the Enumerable class in

System.Linq, there are around 40 query operators, all implemented as static extension methods. These are called *standard query operators*.

NOTE

LINQ also supports sequences that can be dynamically fed from a remote data source such as SQL Server. These sequences additionally implement the IQueryable<> interface and are supported through a matching set of standard query operators in the Queryable class.

A simple query

A *query* is an expression that transforms sequences with one or more query operators. The simplest query comprises one input sequence and one operator. For instance, we can apply the Where operator on a simple array to extract those names whose length is at least four characters, as follows:

```
string[] names = { "Tom", "Dick", "Harry" };

IEnumerable<string> filteredNames =
  System.Linq.Enumerable.Where (
    names, n => n.Length >= 4);

foreach (string n in filteredNames)
  Console.Write (n + "|");              // Dick|Harry|
```

Because the standard query operators are implemented as extension methods, we can call Where directly on names, as though it were an instance method:

```
IEnumerable<string> filteredNames =
  names.Where (n => n.Length >= 4);
```

(For this to compile, you must import the System.Linq namespace with a using directive.) The Where method in System.Linq.Enumerable has the following signature:

```
static IEnumerable<TSource> Where<TSource> (
  this IEnumerable<TSource> source,
  Func<TSource,bool> predicate)
```

source is the *input sequence*; predicate is a delegate that is invoked on each input *element*. The Where method includes all elements in the *output sequence* for which the delegate returns true. Internally, it's implemented with an iterator—here's its source code:

```
foreach (TSource element in source)
  if (predicate (element))
    yield return element;
```

Projecting

Another fundamental query operator is the Select method. This transforms (*projects*) each element in the input sequence with a given lambda expression:

```
string[] names = { "Tom", "Dick", "Harry" };

IEnumerable<string> upperNames =
  names.Select (n => n.ToUpper());

foreach (string n in upperNames)
  Console.Write (n + "|");          // TOM|DICK|HARRY|
```

A query can project into an anonymous type:

```
var query = names.Select (n => new {
                                     Name = n,
                                     Length = n.Length
                                   });
foreach (var row in query)
  Console.WriteLine (row);
```

Here's the result:

```
{ Name = Tom, Length = 3 }
{ Name = Dick, Length = 4 }
{ Name = Harry, Length = 5 }
```

Take and Skip

The original ordering of elements within an input sequence is significant in LINQ. Some query operators rely on this behavior, such as Take, Skip, and Reverse. The Take operator outputs the first x elements, discarding the rest:

```
int[] numbers  = { 10, 9, 8, 7, 6 };
IEnumerable<int> firstThree = numbers.Take (3);
// firstThree is { 10, 9, 8 }
```

The Skip operator ignores the first x elements and outputs the rest:

```
IEnumerable<int> lastTwo = numbers.Skip (3);
```

From .NET 6, there are also TakeLast and SkipLast methods, which take or skip the last n elements. Additionally, the Take method has been overloaded to accept a Range variable. This overload can subsume the functionality of all four methods; for instance, Take(5..) is equivalent to Skip(5), and Take(..^5) is equivalent to SkipLast(5).

Element operators

Not all query operators return a sequence. The *element* operators extract one element from the input sequence; examples are First, Last, Single, and ElementAt:

```
int[] numbers      = { 10, 9, 8, 7, 6 };
int firstNumber    = numbers.First();              // 10
int lastNumber     = numbers.Last();               // 6
int secondNumber   = numbers.ElementAt (2);        // 8
int firstOddNum    = numbers.First (n => n%2 == 1); // 9
```

All of these operators throw an exception if no elements are present. To avoid the exception, use FirstOrDefault, LastOrDefault, SingleOrDefault, or ElementAtOrDefault—these return null (or the default value for value types) when no element is found.

The Single and SingleOrDefault methods are equivalent to First and FirstOrDefault except that they throw an exception if there's more than one match. This behavior is useful when you're querying a database table for a row by primary key.

From .NET 6, there are also `MinBy` and `MaxBy` methods, which return the element with the lowest or highest value, as determined by a key selector:

```
string[] names = { "Tom", "Dick", "Harry" };
Console.Write (names.MaxBy (n => n.Length));  // Harry
```

Aggregation operators

The *aggregation* operators return a scalar value, usually of numeric type. The most commonly used aggregation operators are `Count`, `Min`, `Max`, and `Average`:

```
int[] numbers = { 10, 9, 8, 7, 6 };
int count      = numbers.Count();         // 5
int min        = numbers.Min();           // 6
int max        = numbers.Max();           // 10
double avg     = numbers.Average();       // 8
```

`Count` accepts an optional predicate, which indicates whether to include a given element. The following counts all even numbers:

```
int evenNums = numbers.Count (n => n % 2 == 0);   // 3
```

The `Min`, `Max`, and `Average` operators accept an optional argument that transforms each element prior to it being aggregated:

```
int maxRemainderAfterDivBy5 = numbers.Max
                             (n => n % 5);        // 4
```

The following calculates the root mean square of `numbers`:

```
double rms = Math.Sqrt (numbers.Average (n => n * n));
```

Quantifiers

The *quantifiers* return a `bool` value. The quantifiers are `Con tains`, `Any`, `All`, and `SequenceEquals` (which compares two sequences):

```
int[] numbers = { 10, 9, 8, 7, 6 };

bool hasTheNumberNine = numbers.Contains (9);      // true
bool hasMoreThanZeroElements = numbers.Any();      // true
bool hasOddNum = numbers.Any (n => n % 2 == 1);    // true
bool allOddNums = numbers.All (n => n % 2 == 1);   // false
```

Set operators

The *set* operators accept two same-typed input sequences. Con
cat appends one sequence to another; Union does the same but
with duplicates removed:

```
int[] seq1 = { 1, 2, 3 }, seq2 = { 3, 4, 5 };

IEnumerable<int>
  concat = seq1.Concat (seq2),   // { 1, 2, 3, 3, 4, 5 }
  union  = seq1.Union  (seq2),   // { 1, 2, 3, 4, 5 }
```

The other two operators in this category are Intersect and
Except:

```
IEnumerable<int>
  commonality = seq1.Intersect (seq2),   // { 3 }
  difference1 = seq1.Except    (seq2),   // { 1, 2 }
  difference2 = seq2.Except    (seq1);   // { 4, 5 }
```

From .NET 6, there are also set operators that take a key selector (UnionBy, ExceptBy, IntersectBy). The key selector is used
in determining whether an element counts as a duplicate:

```
string[] seq1 = { "A", "b", "C" };
string[] seq2 = { "a", "B", "c" };
var union = seq1.UnionBy (seq2, x => x.ToUpper());
// union is { "A", "b", "C" }
```

Deferred Execution

An important feature of many query operators is that they
execute not when constructed but when *enumerated* (in other
words, when MoveNext is called on its enumerator). Consider
the following query:

```
var numbers = new List<int> { 1 };

IEnumerable<int> query = numbers.Select (n => n * 10);
numbers.Add (2);     // Sneak in an extra element

foreach (int n in query)
  Console.Write (n + "|");              // 10|20|
```

The extra number that we sneaked into the list *after* constructing the query is included in the result because it's not until the `foreach` statement runs that any filtering or sorting takes place. This is called *deferred* or *lazy* evaluation. Deferred execution decouples query *construction* from query *execution*, allowing you to construct a query in several steps, as well as making it possible to query a database without retrieving all the rows to the client. All standard query operators provide deferred execution, with the following exceptions:

- Operators that return a single element or scalar value (the *element operators*, *aggregation operators*, and *quantifiers*)

- The *conversion* operators ToArray, ToList, ToDictionary, ToLookup, and ToHashSet

The conversion operators are handy, in part because they defeat lazy evaluation. This can be useful to "freeze" or cache the results at a certain point in time, to avoid re-executing a computationally intensive or remotely sourced query such as an Entity Framework table. (A side effect of lazy evaluation is that the query is reevaluated should you later re-enumerate it.)

The following example illustrates the ToList operator:

```
var numbers = new List<int>() { 1, 2 };

List<int> timesTen = numbers
  .Select (n => n * 10)
  .ToList();     // Executes immediately into a List<int>

numbers.Clear();
Console.WriteLine (timesTen.Count);       // Still 2
```

WARNING

Subqueries provide another level of indirection. Everything in a subquery is subject to deferred execution, including aggregation and conversion methods, because the subquery is itself executed only lazily upon demand. Assuming names is a string array, a subquery looks like this:

```
names.Where (
  n => n.Length ==
    names.Min (n2 => n2.Length))
```

Standard Query Operators

We can divide the standard query operators (as implemented in the System.Linq.Enumerable class) into 12 categories, as summarized in Table 1.

Table 1. Query operator categories

Category	Description	Deferred execution?
Filtering	Returns a subset of elements that satisfy a given condition	Yes
Projecting	Transforms each element with a lambda function, optionally expanding subsequences	Yes
Joining	Meshes elements of one collection with another, using a time-efficient lookup strategy	Yes
Ordering	Returns a reordering of a sequence	Yes
Grouping	Groups a sequence into subsequences	Yes
Set	Accepts two same-typed sequences and returns their commonality, sum, or difference	Yes
Element	Picks a single element from a sequence	No
Aggregation	Performs a computation over a sequence, returning a scalar value (typically a number)	No

Category	Description	Deferred execution?
Quantification	Performs a computation over a sequence, returning true or false	No
Conversion: Import	Converts a nongeneric sequence to a (queryable) generic sequence	Yes
Conversion: Export	Converts a sequence to an array, list, dictionary, or lookup, forcing immediate evaluation	No
Generation	Manufactures a simple sequence	Yes

Tables 2 through 13 summarize each query operator. The operators shown in bold have special support in C# (see "Query Expressions" on page 205).

Table 2. Filtering operators

Method	Description
Where	Returns a subset of elements that satisfy a given condition
Take	Returns the first *x* elements, and discards the rest
Skip	Ignores the first *x* elements, and returns the rest
TakeLast	Returns the last *x* elements, and discards the rest
SkipLast	Ignores the last *x* elements, and returns the rest
TakeWhile	Emits elements from the input sequence until the given predicate is true
SkipWhile	Ignores elements from the input sequence until the given predicate is true and then emits the rest
Distinct, DistinctBy	Returns a collection that excludes duplicates

Table 3. Projection operators

Method	Description
Select	Transforms each input element with a given lambda expression
SelectMany	Transforms each input element and then flattens and concatenates the resultant subsequences

Table 4. Joining operators

Method	Description
Join	Applies a lookup strategy to match elements from two collections, emitting a flat result set
GroupJoin	As above, but emits a *hierarchical* result set
Zip	Enumerates two sequences in step, returning a sequence that applies a function over each element pair

Table 5. Ordering operators

Method	Description
OrderBy, ThenBy	Returns the elements sorted in ascending order
OrderByDescending, ThenByDescending	Returns the elements sorted in descending order
Reverse	Returns the elements in reverse order

Table 6. Grouping operators

Method	Description
GroupBy	Groups a sequence into subsequences
Chunk	Groups a sequence into chunks of a given size

Table 7. Set operators

Method	Description
Concat	Concatenates two sequences
Union, UnionBy	Concatenates two sequences, removing duplicates

Method	Description
Intersect, IntersectBy	Returns elements present in both sequences
Except, ExceptBy	Returns elements present in the first sequence but not the second

Table 8. Element operators

Method	Description
First, FirstOrDefault	Returns the first element in the sequence, or the first element satisfying a given predicate
Last, LastOrDefault	Returns the last element in the sequence, or the last element satisfying a given predicate
Single, SingleOrDefault	Equivalent to First/FirstOrDefault but throws an exception if there is more than one match
MinBy, MaxBy	Returns the element with the smallest or largest value, as determined by a key selector
ElementAt, ElementAtOrDefault	Returns the element at the specified position
DefaultIfEmpty	Returns a single-value sequence whose value is null or default(TSource) if the sequence has no elements

Table 9. Aggregation operators

Method	Description
Count, LongCount	Returns the total number of elements in the input sequence, or the number of elements satisfying a given predicate
Min, Max	Returns the smallest or largest element in the sequence
Sum, Average	Calculates a numeric sum or average over elements in the sequence
Aggregate	Performs a custom aggregation

Table 10. Quantifiers

Method	Description
Contains	Returns true if the input sequence contains the given element
Any	Returns true if any elements satisfy the given predicate
All	Returns true if all elements satisfy the given predicate
SequenceEqual	Returns true if the second sequence has identical elements to the input sequence

Table 11. Conversion operators (import)

Method	Description
OfType	Converts IEnumerable to IEnumerable<T>, discarding wrongly typed elements
Cast	Converts IEnumerable to IEnumerable<T>, throwing an exception if there are any wrongly typed elements

Table 12. Conversion operators (export)

Method	Description
ToArray	Converts IEnumerable<T> to T[]
ToList	Converts IEnumerable<T> to List<T>
ToDictionary	Converts IEnumerable<T> to Dictionary<TKey,TValue>
ToHashSet	Converts IEnumerable<T> to HashSet<T>
ToLookup	Converts IEnumerable<T> to ILookup<TKey,TElement>
AsEnumerable	Downcasts to IEnumerable<T>
AsQueryable	Casts or converts to IQueryable<T>

Table 13. Generation operators

Method	Description
Empty	Creates an empty sequence
Repeat	Creates a sequence of repeating elements
Range	Creates a sequence of integers

Chaining Query Operators

To build more complex queries, you chain query operators together. For example, the following query extracts all strings containing the letter *a*, sorts them by length, and then converts the results to uppercase:

```
string[] names = { "Tom","Dick","Harry","Mary","Jay" };

IEnumerable<string> query = names
  .Where   (n => n.Contains ("a"))
  .OrderBy (n => n.Length)
  .Select  (n => n.ToUpper());

foreach (string name in query)
  Console.Write (name + "|");

// RESULT: JAY|MARY|HARRY|
```

Where, OrderBy, and Select are all standard query operators that resolve to extension methods in the Enumerable class. The Where operator emits a filtered version of the input sequence, OrderBy emits a sorted version of its input sequence, and Select emits a sequence in which each input element is transformed or *projected* with a given lambda expression (n.ToUpper() in this case). Data flows from left to right through the chain of operators, so the data is first filtered, then sorted, then projected. The end result resembles a production line of conveyor belts, as illustrated in Figure 6.

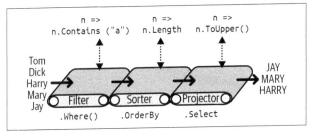

Figure 6. Chaining query operators

Deferred execution is honored throughout with operators, so no filtering, sorting, or projecting takes place until the query is actually enumerated.

Query Expressions

So far, we've written queries by calling extension methods in the Enumerable class. In this book, we describe this as *fluent syntax*. C# also provides special language support for writing queries, called *query expressions*. Here's the preceding query expressed as a query expression:

```
IEnumerable<string> query =
    from n in names
    where n.Contains ("a")
    orderby n.Length
    select n.ToUpper();
```

A query expression always starts with a from clause, and ends with either a select or group clause. The from clause declares a *range variable* (in this case, n), which you can think of as traversing the input collection—rather like foreach. Figure 7 illustrates the complete syntax.

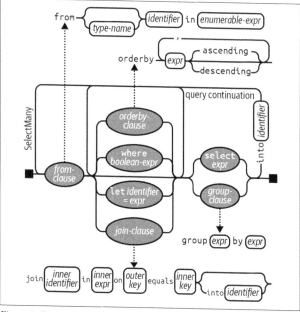

Figure 7. Query expression syntax

NOTE

If you're familiar with SQL, LINQ's query expression syntax—with the from clause first and the select clause last—might look bizarre. Query expression syntax is actually more logical because the clauses appear *in the order they're executed*. This allows Visual Studio to prompt you with IntelliSense as you type and simplifies the scoping rules for subqueries.

The compiler processes query expressions by translating them to fluent syntax. It does this in a fairly mechanical fashion—

much like it translates `foreach` statements into calls to `GetEnum`
`erator` and `MoveNext`:

```
IEnumerable<string> query = names
  .Where   (n => n.Contains ("a"))
  .OrderBy (n => n.Length)
  .Select  (n => n.ToUpper());
```

The `Where`, `OrderBy`, and `Select` operators then resolve using
the same rules that would apply if the query were written
in fluent syntax. In this case, they bind to extension methods in the `Enumerable` class (assuming that you've imported the `System.Linq` namespace) because `names` implements
`IEnumerable<string>`. The compiler doesn't specifically favor
the `Enumerable` class, however, when translating query syntax.
You can think of the compiler as mechanically injecting the
words *Where*, *OrderBy*, and *Select* into the statement and then
compiling it as though you'd typed the method names yourself.
This offers flexibility in how they resolve—the operators in
Entity Framework queries, for instance, bind instead to the
extension methods in the `Queryable` class.

Query expressions versus fluent queries

Query expressions and fluent queries each have advantages.

Query expressions support only a small subset of query operators, namely:

```
Where, Select, SelectMany
OrderBy, ThenBy, OrderByDescending, ThenByDescending
GroupBy, Join, GroupJoin
```

For queries that use other operators, you must either write
entirely in fluent syntax or construct mixed-syntax queries; for
example:

```
string[] names = { "Tom","Dick","Harry","Mary","Jay" };

IEnumerable<string> query =
  from   n in names
  where  n.Length == names.Min (n2 => n2.Length)
  select n;
```

This query returns names whose length matches that of the shortest ("Tom" and "Jay"). The subquery (in bold) calculates the minimum length of each name and evaluates to 3. We need to use fluent syntax for the subquery, because the `Min` operator has no support in query expression syntax. We can, however, still use query syntax for the outer query.

The main advantage of query syntax is that it can radically simplify queries that involve the following:

- A `let` clause for introducing a new variable alongside the range variable
- Multiple generators (`SelectMany`) followed by an outer range variable reference
- A `Join` or `GroupJoin` equivalent followed by an outer range variable reference

The let Keyword

The `let` keyword introduces a new variable alongside the range variable. For instance, suppose that you want to list all names whose length, without vowels, is greater than two characters:

```
string[] names = { "Tom","Dick","Harry","Mary","Jay" };

IEnumerable<string> query =
  from n in names
  let vowelless = Regex.Replace (n, "[aeiou]", "")
  where vowelless.Length > 2
  orderby vowelless
  select n + " - " + vowelless;
```

The output from enumerating this query is:

```
Dick - Dck
Harry - Hrry
Mary - Mry
```

The `let` clause performs a calculation on each element, without losing the original element. In our query, the subsequent clauses (`where`, `orderby`, and `select`) have access to both `n` and vowelless. A query can include multiple let clauses, and they can be interspersed with additional where and join clauses.

The compiler translates the let keyword by projecting into a temporary anonymous type that contains both the original and transformed elements:

```
IEnumerable<string> query = names
 .Select (n => new
   {
     n = n,
     vowelless = Regex.Replace (n, "[aeiou]", "")
   }
 )
 .Where (temp0 => (temp0.vowelless.Length > 2))
 .OrderBy (temp0 => temp0.vowelless)
 .Select (temp0 => ((temp0.n + " - ") + temp0.vowelless))
```

Query Continuations

If you want to add clauses *after* a select or group clause, you must use the into keyword to "continue" the query. For instance:

```
from c in "The quick brown tiger".Split()
select c.ToUpper() into upper
where upper.StartsWith ("T")
select upper

// RESULT: "THE", "TIGER"
```

Following an into clause, the previous range variable is out of scope.

The compiler simply translates queries with an into keyword into a longer chain of operators:

```
"The quick brown tiger".Split()
  .Select (c => c.ToUpper())
  .Where (upper => upper.StartsWith ("T"))
```

(It omits the final Select(upper=>upper) because it's redundant.)

Multiple Generators

A query can include multiple generators (`from` clauses). For example:

```
int[] numbers = { 1, 2, 3 };
string[] letters = { "a", "b" };

IEnumerable<string> query = from n in numbers
                            from l in letters
                            select n.ToString() + l;
```

The result is a cross product, rather like you'd get with nested `foreach` loops:

```
"1a", "1b", "2a", "2b", "3a", "3b"
```

When there's more than one `from` clause in a query, the compiler emits a call to `SelectMany`:

```
IEnumerable<string> query = numbers.SelectMany (
  n => letters,
  (n, l) => (n.ToString() + l));
```

`SelectMany` performs nested looping. It enumerates every element in the source collection (`numbers`), transforming each element with the first lambda expression (`letters`). This generates a sequence of *subsequences*, which it then enumerates. The final output elements are determined by the second lambda expression (`n.ToString()+l`).

If you subsequently apply a `where` clause, you can filter the cross product and project a result akin to a *join*:

```
string[] players = { "Tom", "Jay", "Mary" };

IEnumerable<string> query =
  from name1 in players
  from name2 in players
  where name1.CompareTo (name2) < 0
  orderby name1, name2
  select name1 + " vs " + name2;

RESULT: { "Jay vs Mary", "Jay vs Tom", "Mary vs Tom" }
```

The translation of this query into fluent syntax is more complex, requiring a temporary anonymous projection. The ability to perform this translation automatically is one of the key benefits of query expressions.

The expression in the second generator is allowed to use the first range variable:

```
string[] fullNames =
  { "Anne Williams", "John Fred Smith", "Sue Green" };

IEnumerable<string> query =
  from fullName in fullNames
  from name in fullName.Split()
  select name + " came from " + fullName;

Anne came from Anne Williams
Williams came from Anne Williams
John came from John Fred Smith
```

This works because the expression `fullName.Split` emits a *sequence* (an array of strings).

Multiple generators are used extensively in database queries to flatten parent–child relationships and to perform manual joins.

Joining

LINQ provides three *joining* operators, the main ones being `Join` and `GroupJoin`, which perform keyed lookup-based joins. `Join` and `GroupJoin` support only a subset of the functionality you get with multiple generators/`SelectMany`, but are more performant with local queries because they use a hashtable-based lookup strategy rather than performing nested loops. (With Entity Framework queries, the joining operators have no advantage over multiple generators.)

`Join` and `GroupJoin` support only *equi-joins* (i.e., the joining condition must use the equality operator). There are two methods: `Join` and `GroupJoin`. `Join` emits a flat result set, whereas `GroupJoin` emits a hierarchical result set.

Following is the query expression syntax for a flat join:

```
from outer-var in outer-sequence
join inner-var in inner-sequence
  on outer-key-expr equals inner-key-expr
```

For example, consider the following collections:

```
var customers = new[]
{
  new { ID = 1, Name = "Tom" },
  new { ID = 2, Name = "Dick" },
  new { ID = 3, Name = "Harry" }
};
var purchases = new[]
{
  new { CustomerID = 1, Product = "House" },
  new { CustomerID = 2, Product = "Boat" },
  new { CustomerID = 2, Product = "Car" },
  new { CustomerID = 3, Product = "Holiday" }
};
```

We could perform a join as follows:

```
IEnumerable<string> query =
  from c in customers
  join p in purchases on c.ID equals p.CustomerID
  select c.Name + " bought a " + p.Product;
```

The compiler translates this to:

```
customers.Join (                    // outer collection
  purchases,                        // inner collection
  c => c.ID,                        // outer key selector
  p => p.CustomerID,                // inner key selector
  (c, p) =>                         // result selector
     c.Name + " bought a " + p.Product
);
```

Here's the result:

```
Tom bought a House
Dick bought a Boat
Dick bought a Car
Harry bought a Holiday
```

With local sequences, Join and GroupJoin are more efficient at processing large collections than SelectMany because they first preload the inner sequence into a keyed hashtable-based lookup. With a database query, however, you could achieve the same result equally efficiently as follows:

```
from c in customers
from p in purchases
where c.ID == p.CustomerID
select c.Name + " bought a " + p.Product;
```

GroupJoin

GroupJoin does the same work as Join, but instead of yielding a flat result, it yields a hierarchical result, grouped by each outer element.

The query expression syntax for GroupJoin is the same as for Join, but is followed by the into keyword. Here's a basic example, using the customers and purchases collections we set up in the previous section:

```
var query =
  from c in customers
  join p in purchases on c.ID equals p.CustomerID
  into custPurchases
  select custPurchases;   // custPurchases is a sequence
```

NOTE

An into clause translates to GroupJoin only when it appears directly after a join clause. After a select or group clause, it means *query continuation*. The two uses of the into keyword are quite different, although they have one feature in common: they both introduce a new query variable.

The result is a sequence of sequences—IEnumerable<IEnumerable<T>>—which you could enumerate as follows:

```
foreach (var purchaseSequence in query)
  foreach (var purchase in purchaseSequence)
    Console.WriteLine (purchase.Product);
```

This isn't very useful, however, because `outerSeq` has no reference to the outer customer. More commonly, you'd reference the outer range variable in the projection:

```
from c in customers
join p in purchases on c.ID equals p.CustomerID
into custPurchases
select new { CustName = c.Name, custPurchases };
```

You could obtain the same result (but less efficiently, for local queries) by projecting into an anonymous type that included a subquery:

```
from c in customers
select new
{
  CustName = c.Name,
  custPurchases =
    purchases.Where (p => c.ID == p.CustomerID)
}
```

Zip

`Zip` is the simplest joining operator. It enumerates two sequences in step (like a zipper), returning a sequence based on applying a function over each element pair; thus:

```
int[] numbers = { 3, 5, 7 };
string[] words = { "three", "five", "seven", "ignored" };
IEnumerable<string> zip =
  numbers.Zip (words, (n, w) => n + "=" + w);
```

produces a sequence with the following elements:

```
3=three
5=five
7=seven
```

Extra elements in either input sequence are ignored. `Zip` is not supported when you are querying a database.

Ordering

The `orderby` keyword sorts a sequence. You can specify any number of expressions upon which to sort:

```
string[] names = { "Tom","Dick","Harry","Mary","Jay" };

IEnumerable<string> query = from n in names
                            orderby n.Length, n
                            select n;
```

This sorts first by length and then by name, yielding this result:

```
Jay, Tom, Dick, Mary, Harry
```

The compiler translates the first orderby expression to a call to OrderBy, and subsequent expressions to a call to ThenBy:

```
IEnumerable<string> query = names
  .OrderBy (n => n.Length)
  .ThenBy (n => n)
```

The ThenBy operator *refines* rather than *replaces* the previous sorting.

You can include the descending keyword after any of the orderby expressions:

```
orderby n.Length descending, n
```

This translates to the following:

```
.OrderByDescending (n => n.Length).ThenBy (n => n)
```

NOTE

The ordering operators return an extended type of IEnumerable<T> called IOrderedEnumerable<T>. This interface defines the extra functionality required by the ThenBy operator.

Grouping

GroupBy organizes a flat input sequence into sequences of *groups*. For example, the following groups a sequence of names by their length:

```
string[] names = { "Tom","Dick","Harry","Mary","Jay" };

var query = from name in names
            group name by name.Length;
```

The compiler translates this query into the following:

```
IEnumerable<IGrouping<int,string>> query =
  names.GroupBy (name => name.Length);
```

Here's how to enumerate the result:

```
foreach (IGrouping<int,string> grouping in query)
{
  Console.Write ("\r\n Length=" + grouping.Key + ":");
  foreach (string name in grouping)
    Console.Write (" " + name);
}

 Length=3: Tom Jay
 Length=4: Dick Mary
 Length=5: Harry
```

Enumerable.GroupBy works by reading the input elements into a temporary dictionary of lists so that all elements with the same key end up in the same sublist. It then emits a sequence of *groupings*. A grouping is a sequence with a Key property:

```
public interface IGrouping <TKey,TElement>
  : IEnumerable<TElement>, IEnumerable
{
  // Key applies to the subsequence as a whole
  TKey Key { get; }
}
```

By default, the elements in each grouping are untransformed input elements, unless you specify an elementSelector argument. The following projects each input element to uppercase:

```
from name in names
group name.ToUpper() by name.Length
```

which translates to:

```
names.GroupBy (
  name => name.Length,
  name => name.ToUpper() )
```

The subcollections are not emitted in order of key. GroupBy does no *sorting* (in fact, it preserves the original ordering). To sort, you must add an OrderBy operator (which means first adding an into clause, because group by ordinarily ends a query):

```
from name in names
group name.ToUpper() by name.Length into grouping
orderby grouping.Key
select grouping
```

Query continuations are often used in a group by query. The next query filters out groups that have exactly two matches in them:

```
from name in names
group name.ToUpper() by name.Length into grouping
where grouping.Count() == 2
select grouping
```

NOTE

A where after a group by is equivalent to HAVING in SQL. It applies to each subsequence or grouping as a whole rather than the individual elements.

OfType and Cast

OfType and Cast accept a nongeneric IEnumerable collection and emit a generic IEnumerable<T> sequence that you can subsequently query:

```
var classicList = new System.Collections.ArrayList();
classicList.AddRange ( new int[] { 3, 4, 5 } );
IEnumerable<int> sequence1 = classicList.Cast<int>();
```

This is useful because it allows you to query collections written prior to C# 2.0 (when IEnumerable<T> was introduced), such as ControlCollection in System.Windows.Forms.

Cast and OfType differ in their behavior when encountering an input element that's of an incompatible type: Cast throws an exception, whereas OfType ignores the incompatible element.

The rules for element compatibility follow those of C#'s is operator. Here's the internal implementation of Cast:

```
public static IEnumerable<TSource> Cast <TSource>
            (IEnumerable source)
{
  foreach (object element in source)
    yield return (TSource)element;
}
```

C# supports the Cast operator in query expressions—simply insert the element type immediately after the from keyword:

```
from int x in classicList ...
```

This translates to the following:

```
from x in classicList.Cast <int>() ...
```

Dynamic Binding

Dynamic binding defers *binding*—the process of resolving types, members, and operators—from compile time to runtime. Dynamic binding is useful when at compile time *you* know that a certain function, member, or operator exists, but the *compiler* does not. This commonly occurs when you are interoperating with dynamic languages (such as IronPython) and COM and in scenarios when you might otherwise use reflection.

A dynamic type is declared by using the contextual keyword dynamic:

```
dynamic d = GetSomeObject();
d.Quack();
```

A dynamic type instructs the compiler to relax. We expect the runtime type of d to have a Quack method. We just can't prove it statically. Because d is dynamic, the compiler defers binding Quack to d until runtime. Understanding what this means requires distinguishing between *static binding* and *dynamic binding*.

Static Binding Versus Dynamic Binding

The canonical binding example is mapping a name to a specific function when compiling an expression. To compile the following expression, the compiler needs to find the implementation of the method named Quack:

```
d.Quack();
```

Let's suppose the static type of d is Duck:

```
Duck d = ...
d.Quack();
```

In the simplest case, the compiler does the binding by looking for a parameterless method named Quack on Duck. Failing that, the compiler extends its search to methods taking optional parameters, methods on base classes of Duck, and extension methods that take Duck as its first parameter. If no match is found, you'll get a compilation error. Regardless of what method is bound, the bottom line is that the binding is done by the compiler, and the binding utterly depends on statically knowing the types of the operands (in this case, d). This makes it *static binding*.

Now let's change the static type of d to object:

```
object d = ...
d.Quack();
```

Calling Quack gives us a compilation error because although the value stored in d can contain a method called Quack, the compiler cannot know it given that the only information it has is the type of the variable, which in this case is object. But let's now change the static type of d to dynamic:

```
dynamic d = ...
d.Quack();
```

A `dynamic` type is like `object`—it's equally nondescriptive about a type. The difference is that it lets you use it in ways that aren't known at compile time. A dynamic object binds at runtime based on its runtime type, not its compile-time type. When the compiler sees a dynamically bound expression (which in general is an expression that contains any value of type `dynamic`), it merely packages up the expression such that the binding can be done later at runtime.

At runtime, if a dynamic object implements `IDynamicMeta ObjectProvider`, that interface is used to perform the binding. If not, binding occurs in almost the same way as it would have had the compiler known the dynamic object's runtime type. These two alternatives are called *custom binding* and *language binding*.

Custom Binding

Custom binding occurs when a dynamic object implements `IDy namicMetaObjectProvider` (IDMOP). Although you can implement IDMOP on types that you write in C#, and this is useful to do, the more common case is that you have acquired an IDMOP object from a dynamic language that is implemented in .NET on the Dynamic Language Runtime (DLR), such as IronPython or IronRuby. Objects from those languages implicitly implement IDMOP as a means to directly control the meanings of operations performed on them. Here's a simple example:

```
dynamic d = new Duck();
d.Quack();      // Quack was called
d.Waddle();     // Waddle was called

public class Duck : DynamicObject    // in System.Dynamic
{
  public override bool TryInvokeMember (
    InvokeMemberBinder binder, object[] args,
    out object result)
  {
    Console.WriteLine (binder.Name + " was called");
    result = null;
```

```
        return true;
    }
}
```

The Duck class doesn't actually have a Quack method. Instead, it uses custom binding to intercept and interpret all method calls. We discuss custom binders in detail in *C# 12 in a Nutshell*.

Language Binding

Language binding occurs when a dynamic object does not implement IDynamicMetaObjectProvider. Language binding is useful when you are working around imperfectly designed types or inherent limitations in the .NET type system. For example, the built-in numeric types are imperfect in that they have no common interface. We have seen that methods can be bound dynamically; the same is true for operators:

```
int x = 3, y = 4;
Console.WriteLine (Mean (x, y));

dynamic Mean (dynamic x, dynamic y) => (x+y) / 2;
```

The benefit is obvious—you don't need to duplicate code for each numeric type. However, you lose static type safety, risking runtime exceptions rather than compile-time errors.

NOTE

Dynamic binding circumvents static type safety but not runtime type safety. Unlike with reflection, you cannot circumvent member accessibility rules with dynamic binding.

By design, language runtime binding behaves as similarly as possible to static binding, had the runtime types of the dynamic objects been known at compile time. In the previous example, the behavior of our program would be identical if we hardcoded Mean to work with the int type. The most notable exception in parity between static and dynamic binding is for extension methods, which we discuss in "Uncallable Functions" on page 226.

NOTE

Dynamic binding also incurs a performance hit. Because of the DLR's caching mechanisms, however, repeated calls to the same dynamic expression are optimized, allowing you to efficiently call dynamic expressions in a loop. This optimization brings the typical overhead for a simple dynamic expression on today's hardware down to less than 100 ns.

RuntimeBinderException

If a member fails to bind, a `RuntimeBinderException` is thrown. You can think of this as a compile-time error at runtime:

```
dynamic d = 5;
d.Hello();        // throws RuntimeBinderException
```

The exception is thrown because the int type has no `Hello` method.

Runtime Representation of dynamic

There is a deep equivalence between the `dynamic` and `object` types. The runtime treats the following expression as `true`:

```
typeof (dynamic) == typeof (object)
```

This principle extends to constructed types and array types:

```
typeof (List<dynamic>) == typeof (List<object>)
typeof (dynamic[]) == typeof (object[])
```

Like an object reference, a dynamic reference can point to an object of any type (except pointer types):

```
dynamic x = "hello";
Console.WriteLine (x.GetType().Name);  // String
```

```
x = 123;   // No error (despite same variable)
Console.WriteLine (x.GetType().Name);   // Int32
```

Structurally, there is no difference between an object reference and a dynamic reference. A dynamic reference simply enables dynamic operations on the object it points to. You can convert from object to dynamic to perform any dynamic operation you want on an object:

```
object o = new System.Text.StringBuilder();
dynamic d = o;
d.Append ("hello");
Console.WriteLine (o);   // hello
```

Dynamic Conversions

The dynamic type has implicit conversions to and from all other types. For a conversion to succeed, the runtime type of the dynamic object must be implicitly convertible to the target static type.

The following example throws a RuntimeBinderException because an int is not implicitly convertible to a short:

```
int i = 7;
dynamic d = i;
long l = d;      // OK - implicit conversion works
short j = d;     // throws RuntimeBinderException
```

var Versus dynamic

The var and dynamic types bear a superficial resemblance, but the difference is deep:

- var says, "Let the *compiler* figure out the type."
- dynamic says, "Let the *runtime* figure out the type."

To illustrate:

```
dynamic x = "hello";  // Static type is dynamic
var y = "hello";      // Static type is string
int i = x;            // Runtime error
int j = y;            // Compile-time error
```

Dynamic Expressions

Fields, properties, methods, events, constructors, indexers, operators, and conversions can all be called dynamically.

Trying to consume the result of a dynamic expression with a void return type is prohibited—just as with a statically typed expression. The difference is that the error occurs at runtime.

Expressions involving dynamic operands are typically themselves dynamic, since the effect of absent type information is cascading:

```
dynamic x = 2;
var y = x * 3;        // Static type of y is dynamic
```

There are a couple of obvious exceptions to this rule. First, casting a dynamic expression to a static type yields a static expression. Second, constructor invocations always yield static expressions—even when called with dynamic arguments.

In addition, there are a few edge cases for which an expression containing a dynamic argument is static, including passing an index to an array and delegate creation expressions.

Dynamic Member Overload Resolution

The canonical use case for dynamic involves a dynamic *receiver*. This means that a dynamic object is the receiver of a dynamic function call:

```
dynamic x = ...;
x.Foo (123);          // x is the receiver
```

However, dynamic binding is not limited to receivers: the method arguments are also eligible for dynamic binding. The effect of calling a function with dynamic arguments is to defer overload resolution from compile time to runtime:

```
static void Foo (int x)    => Console.WriteLine ("int");
static void Foo (string x) => Console.WriteLine ("str");

static void Main()
{
```

```
  dynamic x = 5;
  dynamic y = "watermelon";

  Foo (x);     // int
  Foo (y);     // str
}
```

Runtime overload resolution is also called *multiple dispatch* and is useful in implementing design patterns such as *visitor*.

If a dynamic receiver is not involved, the compiler can statically perform a basic check to see whether the dynamic call will succeed: it checks that a function with the right name and number of parameters exists. If no candidate is found, you get a compile-time error.

If a function is called with a mixture of dynamic and static arguments, the final choice of method will reflect a mixture of dynamic and static binding decisions:

```
static void X(object x, object y) =>Console.Write("oo");
static void X(object x, string y) =>Console.Write("os");
static void X(string x, object y) =>Console.Write("so");
static void X(string x, string y) =>Console.Write("ss");

static void Main()
{
  object o = "hello";
  dynamic d = "goodbye";
  X (o, d);                 // os
}
```

The call to X(o,d) is dynamically bound because one of its arguments, d, is dynamic. But because o is statically known, the binding—even though it occurs dynamically—will make use of that. In this case, overload resolution will pick the second implementation of X due to the static type of o and the runtime type of d. In other words, the compiler is "as static as it can possibly be."

Uncallable Functions

Some functions cannot be called dynamically. You cannot call the following:

- Extension methods (via extension method syntax)
- Any member of an interface (via the interface)
- Base members hidden by a subclass

This is because dynamic binding requires two pieces of information: the name of the function to call, and the object upon which to call the function. However, in each of the three uncallable scenarios, an *additional type* is involved, which is known only at compile time. And there is no way to specify these additional types dynamically.

When you are calling extension methods, that additional type is an extension class, chosen implicitly by virtue of `using` directives in your source code (which disappear after compilation). When calling members via an interface, you communicate the additional type via an implicit or explicit cast. (With explicit implementation, it's in fact impossible to call a member without casting to the interface.) A similar situation arises when you are calling a hidden base member: you must specify an additional type via either a cast or the `base` keyword—and that additional type is lost at runtime.

Operator Overloading

You can overload operators to provide more natural syntax for custom types. Operator overloading is most appropriately used for implementing custom structs that represent fairly primitive data types. For example, a custom numeric type is an excellent candidate for operator overloading.

You can overload the following symbolic operators:

```
+    -    *    /    ++    --    !    ~    %    &    |    ^
==   !=   <    <<   >>    >
```

You can override implicit and explicit conversions (with the `implicit` and `explicit` keywords), as you can the `true` and `false` operators.

The compound assignment operators (e.g., +=, /=) are automatically overridden when you override the noncompound operators (e.g., +, /).

Operator Functions

To overload an operator, you declare an *operator function*. An operator function must be static, and at least one of the operands must be the type in which the operator function is declared.

In the following example, we define a struct called `Note`, representing a musical note, and then overload the + operator:

```
public struct Note
{
  int value;

  public Note (int semitonesFromA)
    => value = semitonesFromA;

  public static Note operator + (Note x, int semitones)
    => new Note (x.value + semitones);
}
```

This overload allows us to add an `int` to a `Note`:

```
Note B = new Note (2);
Note CSharp = B + 2;
```

Because we overrode +, we can use += too:

```
CSharp += 2;
```

From C# 11, you can also declare a checked version that will be called inside checked expressions or blocks. These are called *checked operators*:

```
public static Note operator checked + (Note x, int semis)
  => checked (new Note (x.value + semis));
```

Overloading Equality and Comparison Operators

Equality and comparison operators are often overridden when writing structs, and in rare cases with classes. Special rules and obligations apply when overloading these operators:

Pairing
> The C# compiler enforces that operators that are logical pairs are both defined. These operators are (== !=), (< >), and (<= >=).

Equals *and* GetHashCode
> If you overload == and !=, you will usually need to override object's Equals and GetHashCode methods so that collections and hashtables will work reliably with the type.

IComparable *and* IComparable<T>
> If you overload < and >, you would also typically implement IComparable and IComparable<T>.

Extending the previous example, here's how you could overload Note's equality operators:

```
public static bool operator == (Note n1, Note n2)
  => n1.value == n2.value;

public static bool operator != (Note n1, Note n2)
  => !(n1.value == n2.value);

public override bool Equals (object otherNote)
{
  if (!(otherNote is Note)) return false;
  return this == (Note)otherNote;
}
// value's hashcode will work for our own hashcode:
public override int GetHashCode() => value.GetHashCode();
```

Custom Implicit and Explicit Conversions

Implicit and explicit conversions are overloadable operators. These conversions are typically overloaded to make converting between strongly related types (such as numeric types) concise and natural.

As explained in the discussion on types, the rationale behind implicit conversions is that they should always succeed and not lose information during conversion. Otherwise, explicit conversions should be defined.

In the following example, we define conversions between our musical Note type and a double (which represents the frequency in hertz of that note):

```
...
// Convert to hertz
public static implicit operator double (Note x)
  => 440 * Math.Pow (2,(double) x.value / 12 );

// Convert from hertz (accurate to nearest semitone)
public static explicit operator Note (double x)
  => new Note ((int) (0.5 + 12 * (Math.Log(x/440)
              / Math.Log(2)) ));
...

Note n =(Note)554.37;   // explicit conversion
double x = n;           // implicit conversion
```

NOTE

This example is somewhat contrived: in real life, these conversions might be better implemented with a ToFrequency method and a (static) FromFrequency method.

Custom conversions are ignored by the as and is operators.

Attributes

You're already familiar with the notion of attributing code elements of a program with modifiers, such as virtual or ref. These constructs are built into the language. *Attributes* are an extensible mechanism for adding custom information to code elements (assemblies, types, members, return values, and parameters). This extensibility is useful for services that integrate deeply into the type system, without requiring special keywords or constructs in the C# language.

Attribute Classes

An attribute is defined by a class that inherits (directly or indirectly) from the abstract class System.Attribute. To attach an attribute to a code element, specify the attribute's type name in square brackets, before the code element. For example, the following attaches ObsoleteAttribute to the Foo class:

```
[ObsoleteAttribute]
public class Foo {...}
```

This particular attribute is recognized by the compiler and will cause compiler warnings if a type or member marked obsolete is referenced. By convention, all attribute types end with the word *Attribute*. C# recognizes this and allows you to omit the suffix when attaching an attribute:

```
[Obsolete]
public class Foo {...}
```

ObsoleteAttribute is a type declared in the System namespace as follows (simplified for brevity):

```
public sealed class ObsoleteAttribute : Attribute {...}
```

Named and Positional Attribute Parameters

Attributes can have parameters. In the following example, we apply XmlElementAttribute to a class. This attribute instructs XmlSerializer (in System.Xml.Serialization) how an object is represented in XML and accepts several *attribute parameters*. The following attribute maps the CustomerEntity class to an XML element named Customer, belonging to the http://oreilly.com namespace:

```
[XmlElement ("Customer", Namespace="http://oreilly.com")]
public class CustomerEntity { ... }
```

Attribute parameters fall into one of two categories: positional or named. In the preceding example, the first argument is a *positional parameter*; the second is a *named parameter*. Positional parameters correspond to parameters of the attribute type's public constructors. Named parameters correspond to public fields or public properties on the attribute type.

When specifying an attribute, you must include positional parameters that correspond to one of the attribute's constructors. Named parameters are optional.

Attribute Targets

Implicitly, the target of an attribute is the code element it immediately precedes, which is typically a type or type member. You can also attach attributes, however, to an assembly. This requires that you explicitly specify the attribute's target. Here's an example of using the CLSCompliant attribute to specify Common Language Specification (CLS) compliance for an entire assembly:

```
[assembly:CLSCompliant(true)]
```

From C# 10, you can apply attributes to the method, parameters, and return value of a lambda expression:

```
Action<int> a =
  [Description ("Method")]
  [return: Description ("Return value")]
  ([Description ("Parameter")]int x) => Console.Write (x);
```

Specifying Multiple Attributes

You can specify multiple attributes for a single code element. You can list each attribute either within the same pair of square brackets (separated by a comma) or in separate pairs of square brackets (or a combination of the two). The following two examples are semantically identical:

```
[Serializable, Obsolete, CLSCompliant(false)]
public class Bar {...}

[Serializable] [Obsolete] [CLSCompliant(false)]
public class Bar {...}
```

Writing Custom Attributes

You can define your own attributes by subclassing System .Attribute. For example, you could use the following custom attribute for flagging a method for unit testing:

```
[AttributeUsage (AttributeTargets.Method)]
public sealed class TestAttribute : Attribute
{
  public int     Repetitions;
  public string  FailureMessage;

  public TestAttribute () : this (1) { }
  public TestAttribute (int repetitions)
    => Repetitions = repetitions;
}
```

Here's how you could apply the attribute:

```
class Foo
{
  [Test]
  public void Method1() { ... }

  [Test(20)]
  public void Method2() { ... }

  [Test(20, FailureMessage="Debugging Time!")]
  public void Method3() { ... }
}
```

AttributeUsage is itself an attribute that indicates the construct (or combination of constructs) to which the custom attribute can be applied. The AttributeTargets enum includes such members as Class, Method, Parameter, and Constructor (as well as All, which combines all targets).

Retrieving Attributes at Runtime

There are two standard ways to retrieve attributes at runtime:

- Call GetCustomAttributes on any Type or MemberInfo object

- Call `Attribute.GetCustomAttribute` or `Attribute.Get` `CustomAttributes`

These latter two methods are overloaded to accept any reflection object that corresponds to a valid attribute target (`Type`, `Assembly`, `Module`, `MemberInfo`, or `ParameterInfo`).

Here's how we can enumerate each method in the preceding `Foo` class that has a `TestAttribute`:

```
foreach (MethodInfo mi in typeof (Foo).GetMethods())
{
  TestAttribute att = (TestAttribute)
    Attribute.GetCustomAttribute
     (mi, typeof (TestAttribute));

  if (att != null)
    Console.WriteLine (
      "{0} will be tested; reps={1}; msg={2}",
      mi.Name, att.Repetitions, att.FailureMessage);
}
```

Here's the output:

```
Method1 will be tested; reps=1; msg=
Method2 will be tested; reps=20; msg=
Method3 will be tested; reps=20; msg=Debugging Time!
```

Caller Info Attributes

You can tag optional parameters with one of three *caller info attributes*, which instruct the compiler to feed information obtained from the caller's source code into the parameter's default value:

- [`CallerMemberName`] applies the caller's member name.
- [`CallerFilePath`] applies the path to the caller's source code file.
- [`CallerLineNumber`] applies the line number in the caller's source code file.

The `Foo` method in the following program demonstrates all three:

```
using System;
using System.Runtime.CompilerServices;

class Program
{
  static void Main() => Foo();

  static void Foo (
    [CallerMemberName] string memberName = null,
    [CallerFilePath] string filePath = null,
    [CallerLineNumber] int lineNumber = 0)
  {
    Console.WriteLine (memberName);
    Console.WriteLine (filePath);
    Console.WriteLine (lineNumber);
  }
}
```

Assuming that our program resides in *c:\source\test\Program.cs*, the output would be:

```
Main
c:\source\test\Program.cs
6
```

As with standard optional parameters, the substitution is done at the *calling site*. Hence, our `Main` method is syntactic sugar for this:

```
static void Main()
  => Foo ("Main", @"c:\source\test\Program.cs", 6);
```

Caller info attributes are useful for writing logging functions and for implementing change notification patterns. For instance, we can call a method such as the following from within a property's `set` accessor—without having to specify the property's name:

```
void RaisePropertyChanged (
  [CallerMemberName] string propertyName = null)
{
  ...
}
```

CallerArgumentExpression

A method parameter to which you apply the [CallerArgumen
tExpression] attribute captures an argument expression from
the call site:

```
Print (Math.PI * 2);

void Print (double number,
  [CallerArgumentExpression("number")] string expr = null)
    => Console.WriteLine (expr);

// Output: Math.PI * 2
```

The main application for this feature is when writing validation
and assertion libraries. In the following example, an exception
is thrown, whose message includes the text "2 + 2 == 5." This
aids in debugging:

```
Assert (2 + 2 == 5);

void Assert (bool condition,
  [CallerArgumentExpression ("condition")]
  string msg = null)
{
  if (!condition)
    throw new Exception ("Assert failed: " + msg);
}
```

You can use [CallerArgumentExpression] multiple times in
order to capture multiple argument expressions.

Asynchronous Functions

The await and async keywords support *asynchronous programming*, a style of programming in which long-running functions
do most or all of their work *after* returning to the caller. This
is in contrast to normal *synchronous* programming, in which
long-running functions *block* the caller until the operation
is complete. Asynchronous programming implies *concurrency*
because the long-running operation continues *in parallel* to the
caller. The implementer of an asynchronous function initiates
this concurrency either through multithreading (for compute-

bound operations) or via a callback mechanism (for I/O-bound operations).

NOTE

Multithreading, concurrency, and asynchronous programming are large topics. We dedicate two chapters to them in *C# 12 in a Nutshell* and discuss them online at *http://albahari.com/threading*.

For instance, consider the following *synchronous* method, which is long-running and compute-bound:

```
int ComplexCalculation()
{
  double x = 2;
  for (int i = 1; i < 100000000; i++)
    x += Math.Sqrt (x) / i;
  return (int)x;
}
```

This method blocks the caller for a few seconds while it runs, before returning the result of the calculation to the caller:

```
int result = ComplexCalculation();
// Sometime later:
Console.WriteLine (result);   // 116
```

The CLR defines a class called Task<TResult> (in System.Threading.Tasks) to encapsulate the concept of an operation that completes in the future. You can generate a Task<TResult> for a compute-bound operation by calling Task.Run, which instructs the CLR to run the specified delegate on a separate thread that executes in parallel to the caller:

```
Task<int> ComplexCalculationAsync()
  => Task.Run ( () => ComplexCalculation() );
```

This method is *asynchronous* because it returns immediately to the caller while it executes concurrently. However, we need some mechanism to allow the caller to specify what should happen when the operation finishes and the result becomes available. Task<TResult> solves this by exposing a GetAwaiter method that lets the caller attach a *continuation*:

```
Task<int> task = ComplexCalculationAsync();
var awaiter = task.GetAwaiter();
awaiter.OnCompleted (() =>        // Continuation
{
  int result = awaiter.GetResult();
  Console.WriteLine (result);      // 116
});
```

This says to the operation, "When you finish, execute the specified delegate." Our continuation first calls GetResult, which returns the result of the calculation. (Or, if the task *faulted*—threw an exception—calling GetResult rethrows that exception.) Our continuation then writes out the result via Console.WriteLine.

The await and async Keywords

The await keyword simplifies the attaching of continuations. Starting with a basic scenario, consider the following:

```
var result = await expression;
statement(s);
```

The compiler expands this into something functionally similar to the following:

```
var awaiter = expression.GetAwaiter();
awaiter.OnCompleted (() =>
{
  var result = awaiter.GetResult();
  statement(s);
});
```

Hence, we can call the `ComplexCalculationAsync` method we defined previously, like this:

```
int result = await ComplexCalculationAsync();
Console.WriteLine (result);
```

To compile, we need to add the async modifier to the containing method:

```
async void Test()
{
  int result = await ComplexCalculationAsync();
  Console.WriteLine (result);
}
```

The async modifier instructs the compiler to treat await as a keyword rather than an identifier should an ambiguity arise within that method (this ensures that code written prior to C# 5.0 that might use await as an identifier will still compile without error). The async modifier can be applied only to methods (and lambda expressions) that return void or (as you'll see later) a Task or Task<TResult>.

Methods with the `async` modifier are called *asynchronous functions* because they themselves are typically asynchronous. To see why, let's look at how execution proceeds through an asynchronous function.

Upon encountering an `await` expression, execution (normally) returns to the caller—rather like with `yield return` in an iterator. But before returning, the runtime attaches a continuation to the awaited task, ensuring that when the task completes, execution jumps back into the method and continues where it left off. If the task faults, its exception is rethrown (by virtue of calling `GetResult`); otherwise, its return value is assigned to the `await` expression.

NOTE

The CLR's implementation of a task awaiter's `OnComple ted` method ensures that by default, continuations are posted through the current *synchronization context*, if one is present. In practice, this means that in rich-client UI scenarios (WPF, WinUI, and Windows Forms), if you `await` on a UI thread, your code will continue on that same thread. This simplifies thread safety.

The expression upon which you `await` is typically a task; however, any object with a `GetAwaiter` method that returns an *awaitable object*—implementing `INotifyComple tion.OnCompleted` and with an appropriately typed `GetResult` method (and a `bool IsCompleted` property that tests for synchronous completion)—will satisfy the compiler.

Notice that our `await` expression evaluates to an `int` type; this is because the expression that we awaited was a `Task<int>` (whose `GetAwaiter().GetResult()` method returns an `int`).

Awaiting a nongeneric task is legal and generates a void expression:

```
await Task.Delay (5000);
Console.WriteLine ("Five seconds passed!");
```

`Task.Delay` is a static method that returns a `Task` that completes in the specified number of milliseconds. The *synchronous* equivalent of `Task.Delay` is `Thread.Sleep`.

`Task` is the nongeneric base class of `Task<TResult>` and is functionally equivalent to `Task<TResult>` except that it has no result.

Capturing Local State

The real power of `await` expressions is that they can appear almost anywhere in code. Specifically, an `await` expression can appear in place of any expression (within an asynchronous function) except for within a `lock` statement or `unsafe` context.

In the following example, we `await` within a loop:

```
async void Test()
{
  for (int i = 0; i < 10; i++)
  {
    int result = await ComplexCalculationAsync();
    Console.WriteLine (result);
  }
}
```

Upon first executing `ComplexCalculationAsync`, execution returns to the caller by virtue of the `await` expression. When the method completes (or faults), execution resumes where it left off, with the values of local variables and loop counters preserved. The compiler achieves this by translating such code into a state machine, like it does with iterators.

Without the `await` keyword, the manual use of continuations means that you must write something equivalent to a state machine. This is traditionally what makes asynchronous programming difficult.

Writing Asynchronous Functions

With any asynchronous function, you can replace the void return type with a Task to make the method itself *usefully* asynchronous (and awaitable). No further changes are required:

```
async Task PrintAnswerToLife()
{
  await Task.Delay (5000);
  int answer = 21 * 2;
  Console.WriteLine (answer);
}
```

Notice that we don't explicitly return a task in the method body. The compiler manufactures the task, which it signals upon completion of the method (or upon an unhandled exception). This makes it easy to create asynchronous call chains:

```
async Task Go()
{
  await PrintAnswerToLife();
  Console.WriteLine ("Done");
}
```

(And because Go returns a Task, Go itself is awaitable.) The compiler expands asynchronous functions that return tasks into code that (indirectly) uses TaskCompletionSource to create a task that it then signals or faults.

NOTE

TaskCompletionSource is a CLR type that lets you create tasks that you manually control, signaling them as complete with a result (or as faulted with an exception). Unlike Task.Run, TaskCompletionSource doesn't tie up a thread for the duration of the operation. It's also used for writing I/O-bound task-returning methods (such as Task.Delay).

The aim is to ensure that when a task-returning asynchronous method finishes, execution can jump back to whoever awaited it, via a continuation.

Returning Task<TResult>

You can return a Task<TResult> if the method body returns TResult:

```
async Task<int> GetAnswerToLife()
{
  await Task.Delay (5000);
  int answer = 21 * 2;
  // answer is int so our method returns Task<int>
  return answer;
}
```

We can demonstrate GetAnswerToLife by calling it from Print AnswerToLife (which is, in turn, called from Go):

```
async Task Go()
{
  await PrintAnswerToLife();
  Console.WriteLine ("Done");
}
async Task PrintAnswerToLife()
{
  int answer = await GetAnswerToLife();
  Console.WriteLine (answer);
}
async Task<int> GetAnswerToLife()
{
  await Task.Delay (5000);
  int answer = 21 * 2;
  return answer;
}
```

Asynchronous functions make asynchronous programming similar to synchronous programming. Here's the synchronous equivalent of our call graph, for which calling Go() gives the same result after blocking for five seconds:

```
void Go()
{
  PrintAnswerToLife();
  Console.WriteLine ("Done");
}
void PrintAnswerToLife()
{
  int answer = GetAnswerToLife();
  Console.WriteLine (answer);
}
int GetAnswerToLife()
{
  Thread.Sleep (5000);
  int answer = 21 * 2;
  return answer;
}
```

This also illustrates the basic principle of how to design with asynchronous functions in C#, which is to write your methods synchronously and then replace *synchronous* method calls with *asynchronous* method calls that you await.

Parallelism

We've just demonstrated the most common pattern, which is to await task-returning functions immediately after calling them. This results in sequential program flow that's logically similar to the synchronous equivalent.

Calling an asynchronous method without awaiting it allows the code that follows to execute in parallel. For example, the following executes PrintAnswerToLife twice, concurrently:

```
var task1 = PrintAnswerToLife();
var task2 = PrintAnswerToLife();
await task1; await task2;
```

By awaiting both operations afterward, we "end" the parallelism at that point (and rethrow any exceptions from those tasks). The Task class provides a static method called WhenAll to achieve the same result slightly more efficiently. WhenAll returns a task that completes when all of the tasks that you pass to it complete:

```
await Task.WhenAll (PrintAnswerToLife(),
                    PrintAnswerToLife());
```

WhenAll is called a *task combinator*. (The Task class also provides a task combinator called WhenAny, which completes when *any* of the tasks provided to it complete.) We cover the task combinators in detail in *C# 12 in a Nutshell.*

Asynchronous Lambda Expressions

We know that ordinary *named* methods can be asynchronous:

```
async Task NamedMethod()
{
  await Task.Delay (1000);
  Console.WriteLine ("Foo");
}
```

So, too, can *unnamed* methods (lambda expressions and anonymous methods), if preceded by the async keyword:

```
Func<Task> unnamed = async () =>
{
  await Task.Delay (1000);
  Console.WriteLine ("Foo");
};
```

You can call and await these in the same way:

```
await NamedMethod();
await unnamed();
```

You can use asynchronous lambda expressions when attaching event handlers:

```
myButton.Click += async (sender, args) =>
{
  await Task.Delay (1000);
  myButton.Content = "Done";
};
```

This is more succinct than the following, which has the same effect:

```
myButton.Click += ButtonHandler;
...
async void ButtonHandler (object sender, EventArgs args)
```

```
{
  await Task.Delay (1000);
  myButton.Content = "Done";
};
```

Asynchronous lambda expressions can also return Task
<TResult>:

```
Func<Task<int>> unnamed = async () =>
{
  await Task.Delay (1000);
  return 123;
};
int answer = await unnamed();
```

Asynchronous Streams

With yield return, you can write an iterator; with await,
you can write an asynchronous function. *Asynchronous streams*
(from C# 8) combine these concepts and let you write an iterator that awaits, yielding elements asynchronously. This support
builds on the following pair of interfaces, which are asynchronous counterparts to the enumeration interfaces we described
in "Enumeration and Iterators" on page 161:

```
public interface IAsyncEnumerable<out T>
{
  IAsyncEnumerator<T> GetAsyncEnumerator (...);
}

public interface IAsyncEnumerator<out T>: IAsyncDisposable
{
  T Current { get; }
  ValueTask<bool> MoveNextAsync();
}
```

ValueTask<T> is a struct that wraps Task<T> and is behaviorally
equivalent to Task<T>, except that it enables more efficient
execution when the task completes synchronously (which can
happen often when enumerating a sequence). IAsyncDisposa
ble is an asynchronous version of IDisposable and provides
an opportunity to perform cleanup should you choose to manually implement the interfaces:

```
public interface IAsyncDisposable
{
  ValueTask DisposeAsync();
}
```

NOTE

The act of fetching each element from the sequence (Move
NextAsync) is an asynchronous operation, so asynchronous streams are suitable when elements arrive in a piece-
meal fashion (such as when processing data from a video
stream). In contrast, the following type is more suitable
when the sequence *as a whole* is delayed, but the elements,
when they arrive, arrive all together:

```
Task<IEnumerable<T>>
```

To generate an asynchronous stream, you write a method that
combines the principles of iterators and asynchronous methods. In other words, your method should include both yield
return and await, and it should return IAsyncEnumerable<T>:

```
async IAsyncEnumerable<int> RangeAsync (
  int start, int count, int delay)
{
  for (int i = start; i < start + count; i++)
  {
    await Task.Delay (delay);
    yield return i;
  }
}
```

To consume an asynchronous stream, use the await foreach
statement:

```
await foreach (var number in RangeAsync (0, 10, 100))
  Console.WriteLine (number);
```

Static Polymorphism

In "Static virtual/abstract interface members" on page 120, we introduced an advanced feature whereby an interface can define `static virtual` or `static abstract` members, which are then implemented as static members by classes and structs. Later, in "Generic Constraints" on page 129, we showed that applying an interface constraint to a type parameter gives a method access to that interface's members. In this section, we'll demonstrate how this enables *static polymorphism*, allowing for features such as generic math.

To illustrate, consider the following interface, which defines a static method to create a random instance of some type T:

```
interface ICreateRandom<T>
{
  static abstract T CreateRandom();
}
```

Suppose now that we wish to implement this interface in the following record:

```
record Point (int X, int Y);
```

With the help of the System.Random class (whose Next method generates a random integer), we can implement the static CreateRandom method as follows:

```
record Point (int X, int Y) : ICreateRandom<Point>
{
  static Random rnd = new();

  public static Point CreateRandom() =>
    new Point (rnd.Next(), rnd.Next());
}
```

To call this method via the interface, we use a *constrained type parameter*. The following method creates an array of test data using this approach:

```
T[] CreateTestData<T> (int count)
  where T : ICreateRandom<T>
{
```

```
    T[] result = new T[count];
    for (int i = 0; i < count; i++)
      result [i] = T.CreateRandom();
    return result;
}
```

This line of code demonstrates its use:

```
Point[] testData = CreateTestData<Point>(50);
```

Our call to the static CreateRandom method in CreateTestData is *polymorphic* because it works not just with Point but with any type that implements ICreateRandom<T>. This is different from *instance* polymorphism, because we don't need an *instance* of ICreateRandom<T> on which to call CreateRandom; we call CreateRandom on the type itself.

Polymorphic Operators

Because operators are essentially static functions (see "Operator Overloading" on page 226), operators can also be declared as static virtual interface members:

```
interface IAddable<T> where T : IAddable<T>
{
    abstract static T operator + (T left, T right);
}
```

NOTE

The *self-referencing* type constraint in this interface definition is necessary to satisfy the compiler's rules for operator overloading. Recall that when defining an operator function, at least one of the operands must be the type in which the operator function is declared. In this example, our operands are of type T, whereas the containing type is IAddable<T>, so we require a self-referencing type constraint to allow T to be treated as IAddable<T>.

Here's how we can implement the interface:

```
record Point (int X, int Y) : IAddable<Point>
{
  public static Point operator +(Point left, Point right)
    => new Point (left.X + right.X, left.Y + right.Y);
}
```

With a constrained type parameter, we can then write a method that calls our addition operator polymorphically (with edge-case handling omitted for brevity):

```
T Sum<T> (params T[] values) where T : IAddable<T>
{
  T total = values[0];
  for (int i = 1; i < values.Length; i++)
    total += values[i];
  return total;
}
```

Our call to the + operator (via the += operator) is polymorphic because it binds to IAddable<T>, not Point. Hence, our Sum method works with all types that implement IAddable<T>.

Of course, an interface such as IAddable<T> would be much more useful if it were defined in the .NET runtime, and if all .NET numeric types implemented it. Fortunately, this is indeed the case from .NET 7: the System.Numerics namespace includes (a more sophisticated version of) IAddable, along with many other arithmetic interfaces—most of which are encompassed by INumber<TSelf>.

Generic Math

Before .NET 7, code that performed arithmetic had to be hard-coded to a particular numeric type such as int or double. From .NET 7, the INumber<TSelf> interface was added to unify arithmetic operations across numeric types, allowing generic methods such as the following to be written:

```
T Sum<T> (params T[] numbers) where T : INumber<T>
{
  T total = T.Zero;
  foreach (T n in numbers)
    total += n;  // Invokes addition for any numeric type
  return total;
```

```
    }

    int intSum = Sum (3, 5, 7);
    double doubleSum = Sum (3.2, 5.3, 7.1);
    decimal decimalSum = Sum (3.2m, 5.3m, 7.1m);
```

INumber<TSelf> is implemented by all real and integral numeric
types in .NET (as well as char). It can be thought of as an
umbrella interface, comprising other more granular interfaces
for each kind of arithmetic operation (addition, subtraction,
multiplication, division, modulus calculation, comparison, and
so on), as well as interfaces for parsing and formatting. These
interfaces define static abstract operators and methods—which
allow the += operator (and the call to T.Zero) to work inside
our Sum method.

Unsafe Code and Pointers

C# supports direct memory manipulation via pointers within
blocks of code marked as unsafe. Pointer types are useful for
interoperating with native APIs, for accessing memory outside
the managed heap, and in implementing micro-optimizations
in performance-critical hotspots.

Projects that include unsafe code must specify <AllowUnsafe
Blocks>true</AllowUnsafeBlocks> in the project file.

Pointer Basics

For every value type or reference type V, there is a corresponding pointer type V*. A pointer instance holds the address of
a variable. Pointer types can be (unsafely) cast to any other
pointer type. Following are the main pointer operators:

Operator	Meaning
&	The *address-of* operator returns a pointer to the address of a variable.
*	The *dereference* operator returns the variable at the address of a pointer.
->	The *pointer-to-member* operator is a syntactic shortcut, in which x->y is equivalent to (*x).y.

Unsafe Code

By marking a type, type member, or statement block with the unsafe keyword, you're permitted to use pointer types and perform C++-style pointer operations on memory within that scope. Here is an example of using pointers to quickly process a bitmap:

```
unsafe void BlueFilter (int[,] bitmap)
{
  int length = bitmap.Length;
  fixed (int* b = bitmap)
  {
    int* p = b;
    for (int i = 0; i < length; i++)
      *p++ &= 0xFF;
  }
}
```

Unsafe code can run faster than a corresponding safe implementation. In this case, the code would have required a nested loop with array indexing and bounds checking. An unsafe C# method can also be faster than calling an external C function because there is no overhead associated with leaving the managed execution environment.

The fixed Statement

The fixed statement is required to pin a managed object such as the bitmap in the previous example. During the execution of a program, many objects are allocated and deallocated from the heap. To avoid unnecessary waste or fragmentation of memory, the garbage collector moves objects around. Pointing to an object is futile if its address could change while referencing it, so the fixed statement instructs the garbage collector to "pin" the object and not move it around. This can have an impact on the efficiency of the runtime, so you should use fixed blocks only briefly, and you should avoid heap allocation within the fixed block.

Within a fixed statement, you can get a pointer to a value type, an array of value types, or a string. In the case of arrays and strings, the pointer will actually point to the first element, which is a value type.

Value types declared inline within reference types require the reference type to be pinned, as follows:

```
Test test = new Test();
unsafe
{
  fixed (int* p = &test.X)   // Pins test
  {
    *p = 9;
  }
  Console.WriteLine (test.X);
}

class Test { public int X; }
```

The Pointer-to-Member Operator

In addition to the & and * operators, C# also provides the C++-style -> operator, which you can use on structs:

```
Test test = new Test();
unsafe
{
  Test* p = &test;
  p->X = 9;
  System.Console.WriteLine (test.X);
}

struct Test { public int X; }
```

The stackalloc Keyword

You can allocate memory in a block on the stack explicitly with the stackalloc keyword. Because it is allocated on the stack, its lifetime is limited to the execution of the method, just as with any other local variable. The block can use the [ ] operator to index into memory:

```
int* a = stackalloc int [10];
for (int i = 0; i < 10; ++i)
  Console.WriteLine (a[i]);   // Print raw memory
```

Fixed-Size Buffers

To allocate a block of memory within a struct, use the fixed keyword:

```
unsafe struct UnsafeUnicodeString
{
  public short Length;
  public fixed byte Buffer[30];
}

unsafe class UnsafeClass
{
  UnsafeUnicodeString uus;

  public UnsafeClass (string s)
  {
    uus.Length = (short)s.Length;
    fixed (byte* p = uus.Buffer)
      for (int i = 0; i < s.Length; i++)
        p[i] = (byte) s[i];
  }
}
```

Fixed-size buffers are not arrays: if Buffer were an array, it would consist of a reference to an object stored on the (managed) heap, rather than 30 bytes within the struct itself.

The fixed keyword is also used in this example to pin the object on the heap that contains the buffer (which will be the instance of UnsafeClass).

void*

A *void pointer* (void*) makes no assumptions about the type of the underlying data and is useful for functions that deal with raw memory. An implicit conversion exists from any pointer type to void*. A void* cannot be dereferenced, and arithmetic operations cannot be performed on void pointers. For example:

```
short[] a = {1,1,2,3,5,8,13,21,34,55};
fixed (short* p = a)
{
  //sizeof returns size of value-type in bytes
  Zap (p, a.Length * sizeof (short));
}
foreach (short x in a)
  Console.WriteLine (x);  // Prints all zeros

unsafe void Zap (void* memory, int byteCount)
{
  byte* b = (byte*) memory;
    for (int i = 0; i < byteCount; i++)
      *b++ = 0;
}
```

Function Pointers

A *function pointer* (from C# 9) is like a delegate but without the indirection of a delegate instance; instead, it points directly to a method. A function pointer points only to static methods, lacks multicast capability, and requires an unsafe context (because it bypasses runtime type safety). Its main purpose is to simplify and optimize interop with unmanaged APIs (we cover interop in *C# 12 in a Nutshell*).

A function pointer type is declared as follows (with the return type appearing last):

```
delegate*<int, char, string, void>
```

This matches a function with this signature:

```
void SomeFunction (int x, char y, string z)
```

The & operator creates a function pointer from a method group. Here's a complete example:

```
unsafe
{
  delegate*<string, int> functionPointer = &GetLength;
  int length = functionPointer ("Hello, world");

  static int GetLength (string s) => s.Length;
}
```

In this example, functionPointer is not an *object* upon which you can call a method such as Invoke (or with a reference to a Target object). Instead, it's a variable that points directly to the target method's address in memory:

```
Console.WriteLine ((IntPtr)functionPointer);
```

Preprocessor Directives

Preprocessor directives supply the compiler with additional information about regions of code. The most common preprocessor directives are the conditional directives, which provide a way to include or exclude regions of code from compilation. For example:

```
#define DEBUG
class MyClass
{
  int x;
  void Foo()
  {
    #if DEBUG
    Console.WriteLine ("Testing: x = {0}", x);
    #endif
  }
  ...
}
```

In this class, the statement in Foo is compiled as conditionally dependent upon the presence of the DEBUG symbol. If we remove the DEBUG symbol, the statement is not compiled. Preprocessor symbols can be defined within a source file (as we have done), or within the `<DefineConstants>` element in a project file.

With the `#if` and `#elif` directives, you can use the `||`, `&&`, and `!` operators to perform *or*, *and*, and *not* operations on multiple symbols. The following directive instructs the compiler to include the code that follows if the TESTMODE symbol is defined and the DEBUG symbol is not defined:

```
#if TESTMODE && !DEBUG
    ...
```

Keep in mind, however, that you're not building an ordinary C# expression, and the symbols upon which you operate have absolutely no connection to *variables*—static or otherwise.

The `#error` and `#warning` symbols prevent accidental misuse of conditional directives by making the compiler generate a warning or error given an undesirable set of compilation symbols.

Table 14 describes the complete list of preprocessor directives.

Table 14. Preprocessor directives

Preprocessor directive	Action
`#define` *symbol*	Defines *symbol*.
`#undef` *symbol*	Undefines *symbol*.
`#if` *symbol* [*operator symbol2*]...	Conditional compilation (*operator*s are `==`, `!=`, `&&`, and `||`).
`#else`	Executes code to subsequent `#endif`.
`#elif` *symbol* [*operator symbol2*]	Combines `#else` branch and `#if` test.
`#endif`	Ends conditional directives.
`#warning` *text*	*text* of the warning to appear in compiler output.
`#error` *text*	*text* of the error to appear in compiler output.

Preprocessor directive	Action
#line [*number* ["*file*"] | hidden]	*number* specifies the line in source code; *file* is the filename to appear in computer output; hidden instructs debuggers to skip over code from this point until the next #line directive.
#region *name*	Marks the beginning of an outline.
#endregion	Ends an outline region.
#pragma warning	See the next section.
#nullable *option*	See "Nullable Reference Types" on page 172.

Pragma Warning

The compiler generates a warning when it spots something in your code that seems unintentional. Unlike errors, warnings don't ordinarily prevent your application from compiling.

Compiler warnings can be extremely valuable in spotting bugs. Their usefulness, however, is undermined when you get *false* warnings. In a large application, maintaining a good signal-to-noise ratio is essential if the "real" warnings are to be noticed.

To this effect, the compiler allows you to selectively suppress warnings with the #pragma warning directive. In this example, we instruct the compiler not to warn us about the field Message not being used:

```
public class Foo
{
  #pragma warning disable 414
  static string Message = "Hello";
  #pragma warning restore 414
}
```

Omitting the number in the #pragma warning directive disables or restores all warning codes.

If you are thorough in applying this directive, you can compile with the /warnaserror switch—this instructs the compiler to treat any residual warnings as errors.

XML Documentation

A *documentation comment* is a piece of embedded XML that documents a type or member. A documentation comment comes immediately before a type or member declaration and starts with three slashes:

```
/// <summary>Cancels a running query.</summary>
public void Cancel() { ... }
```

Multiline comments can be done like this:

```
/// <summary>
/// Cancels a running query
/// </summary>
public void Cancel() { ... }
```

Or like this (notice the extra star at the start):

```
/**
    <summary> Cancels a running query. </summary>
*/
public void Cancel() { ... }
```

If you compile with the /doc directive (or enable XML documentation in the project file), the compiler extracts and collates documentation comments into a single XML file. This has two main uses:

- If placed in the same folder as the compiled assembly, Visual Studio automatically reads the XML file and uses the information to provide IntelliSense member listings to consumers of the assembly of the same name.

- Third-party tools (such as Sandcastle and NDoc) can transform the XML file into an HTML help file.

Standard XML Documentation Tags

Here are the standard XML tags that Visual Studio and documentation generators recognize:

`<summary>`

```
<summary>...</summary>
```

Indicates the tool tip that IntelliSense should display for the type or member. Typically, a single phrase or sentence.

`<remarks>`

```
<remarks>...</remarks>
```

Additional text that describes the type or member. Documentation generators pick this up and merge it into the bulk of a type or member's description.

`<param>`

```
<param name="name">...</param>
```

Explains a parameter on a method.

`<returns>`

```
<returns>...</returns>
```

Explains the return value for a method.

`<exception>`

```
<exception [cref="type"]>...</exception>
```

Lists an exception that a method might throw (`cref` refers to the exception type).

`<permission>`

```
<permission [cref="type"]>...</permission>
```

Indicates an `IPermission` type required by the documented type or member.

`<example>`

```
<example>...</example>
```

Denotes an example (used by documentation generators). This usually contains both description text and source code (source code is typically within a `<c>` or `<code>` tag).

`<c>`

```
<c>...</c>
```

Indicates an inline code snippet. This tag is usually used within an `<example>` block.

`<code>`

```
<code>...</code>
```

Indicates a multiline code sample. This tag is usually used within an `<example>` block.

`<see>`

```
<see cref="member">...</see>
```

Inserts an inline cross-reference to another type or member. HTML documentation generators typically convert this to a hyperlink. The compiler emits a warning if the type or member name is invalid.

`<seealso>`

```
<seealso cref="member">...</seealso>
```

Cross-references another type or member. Documentation generators typically write this into a separate "See Also" section at the bottom of the page.

`<paramref>`

```
<paramref name="name"/>
```

References a parameter from within a `<summary>` or `<remarks>` tag.

`<list>`

```
<list type=[ bullet | number | table ]>
  <listheader>
    <term>...</term>
    <description>...</description>
  </listheader>
  <item>
    <term>...</term>
    <description>...</description>
  </item>
</list>
```

Instructs documentation generators to emit a bulleted, numbered, or table-style list.

`<para>`

```
<para>...</para>
```

Instructs documentation generators to format the contents into a separate paragraph.

`<include>`

```
<include file='filename' path='tagpath[@name="id"]'>
  ...
</include>
```

Merges an external XML file that contains documentation. The path attribute denotes an XPath query to a specific element in that file.

Index

About the Authors

Joseph Albahari is the author of *C# 12 in a Nutshell*, *C# 10 Pocket Reference*, and *LINQ Pocket Reference* (O'Reilly). He also wrote LINQPad—the popular code scratchpad and LINQ querying utility.

Ben Albahari is a former Program Manager at Microsoft, where he worked on Entity Framework and .NET Compact Framework. He also coauthored *C# Essentials* (the first C# book from O'Reilly) and earlier editions of *C# in a Nutshell*.

Colophon

The animal on the cover of *C# 12 Pocket Reference* is a gray crowned crane (*Balearica regulorum*). This bird's range extends from parts of Kenya and Uganda in the north into eastern South Africa, and they prefer to live in habitats such as open marshes and grasslands.

Adult birds stand three to four feet tall and weigh about eight pounds. They are visually striking birds, with a gray body and pale-gray neck, white-and-gold wings, a white face (with a red patch above), a black cap, a bright-red throat lappet, and blue eyes. Topping all of this off (and giving them their name) is the distinctive spray of stiff gold filaments at the back of their heads.

Crowned cranes can live for up to 20 years in the wild, spending most of their waking hours stalking through the grass and hunting for small animals and insects, as well as seeds and grains. They are one of only two types of crane to roost at night in trees, a feat made possible by a prehensile hind toe that allows them to grip branches. These birds produce clutches of up to four eggs; a few hours after hatching, the chicks are able to follow their parents, and the family forages together for food.

Social and talkative, crowned cranes group together in pairs or families, which at times combine into flocks of more than one hundred birds. Like other cranes, they are well known for their elaborate mating dance, which includes elements such as short upward flights, wing flapping, and deep bows.

Despite their wide range, these birds are currently considered endangered, threatened by habitat loss, egg poaching, and pesticide use. Many of the animals on O'Reilly covers are endangered; all of them are important to the world.

The cover illustration is by Karen Montgomery, based on a black-and-white engraving from *Cassell's Natural History* (1896). The cover fonts are Gilroy Semibold and Guardian Sans. The text font is Adobe Minion Pro; the heading font is Adobe Myriad Condensed; and the code font is Dalton Maag's Ubuntu Mono.

O'REILLY®

Learn from experts.
Become one yourself.

Books | Live online courses
Instant answers | Virtual events
Videos | Interactive learning

Get started at oreilly.com.